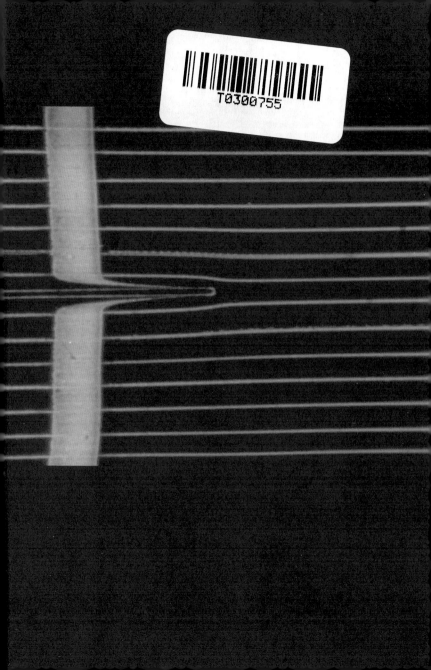

Seldom
Approaches

Also by Syd Staiti
The Undying Present

Seldom
Approaches
Syd Staiti

THE ELEPHANTS

Published 2022 by The Elephants
Printed in the United States
Book design by Aimee C. Harrison
Cover image: "Kingfisher" by Kelly Ording
Interior image: "infinite column (2022)" by arc
The text of this book is set in FreightText Pro

22 23 24 25 26 5 4 3 2 1

First Edition

ISBN 978-1-639551-06-4 (print) and
978-1-988979-46-5 (ebook)

Library of Congress Control Number 2022944340

for Trisha

One

1

Stranded
20

Together
88

This book aims to be only a small fragment of my inner life.

—Jean Genet, *Our Lady of the Flowers*

Seldom
Approaches

one

In the center of a bridge, I'm standing
—standing on the bridge centered—
looking one way and the other

In center, my body is a mass that lies between
water, metal, mud, bone

—that lies between two categories, dead, calcified to the skin—

And the text is a bridge, between
the last thought and the next

In center, a gender—
having traversed the great divide
—no line there—
nothing on the other side
just you

I've stood at the edge of the swamp

surrounded by reeds

waiting for a raft to arrive and take me someplace else

I've gone places on that raft and returned

to the embankment

It is a dream that feels like memory

a dream I want to return to

see where it is that I go

For a year I apply two pumps of gel to my shoulders every day
The regular dose is four
I enjoy the dailyness
Slow progression

The gel is sticky and has a faint, softly chemical smell. I apply it
in the morning, slather it on my shoulders and upper arms. In
the shower the next morning, I scrub off the excess layer before
applying a new coat.

I wear a t-shirt in bed so it doesn't rub off onto the sheets. My
partner can't touch this part of my body. The instructions warn
that any amount of contact with the substance may affect her too.

I track myself closely—
Moods, physical and tonal shifts

As I apply the gel every day—
I live in an apartment in downtown Oakland with my cat. I spend
time with my partner and friends. I go to poetry readings, film
screenings, art events. I sit on the internet. I run around the lake
and do push-ups. I go to work. I read books. I practice *qigong* and
meditation. I think about writing a book alongside myself—not a
book about transition, but a book composed of the writing done
as it's happening.

At the time of writing this, I write:

My body contains both poetry and prose
like a book of dreams
which is akin to dreams
in that the space-time of its reality
is parallel in place to here

I embody a middle place
—the middle place evidenced by my body—
it becomes apparent to some what I'm doing
a shift not only for me, but for others who gaze upon me too

My voice grates and cracks
through the floodlights
as an emergency situation unfolds

Solidifying cells
a voice reverberates
shoulders broad and loose

As the effects are taking shape
my presence exposes the limitations of others

When a shoulder hits into my chest at a rest stop, angry glares
empty stares, vacuous smiles—blank and insincere
to them my body is a blind spot, something they don't understand, have no access to, something over their head, that they
don't know how to reach for

Or the pressure felt when confronted with someone's block
a friend's, I mean—
wanting them to stay with me through it, wanting to reassure
them I'm okay, it's better this way, wanting them to trust it

But finding uncertainty, suspicion, confusion in their eyes or tone
if it's real, they would've known—is what they say, or don't say

My desire to walk them through their walls gently, perhaps even
at my own expense
their inability to acknowledge to me that they're struggling
holding me in a heavier state of remove

What do you say, friend, when you revise me in your mind?

Of course, it could all be in my head
a projection of my own uncertainties. I'm a product of the same
world. same thoughts and suspicions. it's what we've been given.

What do I say, to myself or to another, when I justify a decision to change?

Though I am a more centered self, palms on the bark,
holding my feet
against the ground rooted beneath—

Despite this flurry of unspoken
dialogues in our heads, what are they—?

The conversations we have together
when alone.

At the edge of the embankment

swamp bubbles—

Up on the bridge—gust of wind hits

A stream below, the minnows

swim away to other schools

they stop tuning in with the current

In the dream, there was a place I found—in language

it was mine

After one year of applying the gel
the effects reach a plateau
the slowness begins to feel too slow
I don't want to apply four pumps of gel daily
done with the dailyness
needing to feel action
a desire emerging as need—a need emerging as desire

To do this for no one but myself
Knowing it'll hurt people I love, make them uncomfortable—
a thing I'm not wired for—having always molded myself into
what I think others want me to be

I fear the big intramuscular needle
Learn I can use a smaller one, subcutaneous instead, once a week
Slide the needle into a hefty chunk of skin in my midsection
Say ouch. Fuck. Ow.
From the other room, my partner asks, are you okay?

An hour later, a warm horny energy activates inside me.

At the time of writing it, I write:

I begin to stick a needle into my gut once a week. I get top surgery and tend to the recent scars. I watch as thick hairs emerge on the face, rusty tenor in the voice, enlarged clitoris, more defined muscles. I wonder what I will look like in another year. Wonder if I'll have a book by then—what will it look like?

A year or more has passed, again, since then:

The scars are lighter, the voice drops to a deeper and less metallic tone, facial hair filling in. The text has changed too, a story under construction, in development, tracking its own process, coming closer to what it will be—this—as the body traces its marks.

More time passes, another year or two. Another piece of the book is written.

I have a few hookups with men. I'm calmer, quieter, hairier. The inner rage fades. I learn how to come again, differently, with the loss of the erogenous sensation in my nipples that I relied on in the past. I feel sensitive, quiet, like a man.

I tried to be fierce and strong like a woman, it didn't work. I tried to be non-binary, tried to be a gender-fucker, it didn't work. Despite resisting the category of man and not feeling much like one myself, I learn to settle into the designation, explore what can be done from this place.

I try to write a poem about disagreement
opposition, the language between the two
a placement of parts, self as other
medium and form determining what house, what home

It's more of a push, the birth
I'm pushed into a world by being shoved out from another
or pulled up—out from the sink
by the bloody white-gloved
hands of a misogynist

I slip
out of his grasp and fall into a poem,
bump an elbow on the way down,
land with my foot stuck in the hospital bed railing

The book coming to lay down beside itself, splayed open—
pages in the breeze, dry brittle grassland, skin cells
crisp as a winter chill

In the end, one person begins a process that the other was always
going to start themself
but doesn't

In the end, belongs to one
while the other holds a weight, for having
not done that

There was hair all over the chest, touched
hair on the belly and face

We knew we were alternate
being together we knew
we would part ways also

Body and self
the space there
between the two

In that space no
exact pattern

I resist the urge to spin my life into a story that makes sense
to another.

The story I tell myself privately is real and true
and has nothing to do with sense.

But there is a story I keep longing to tell. Why?
—for what and for who—

Some might find my story disagreeable, or at odds with their
understanding of their own story. As if there is universal cohesion
about such things. As if it would change anything about what's
true of my experience.

A certain kind of storytelling thus steps into the light
a ring surrounding the narrative of a writer
who tells their story with all the details
or tells it all with none—

Who knows the road is long and walks the length of it.

stranded

I arrive on a hill
There are
trees in the
distance
I can't
see
beyond the
boundary
of the trees
but I know
I will
have to get past
them

It is
unclear to me
the differences
between
want
and need
I arrive
without having
to get there
I walk
on the path
through the
checkpoint

the gate
where they
check
our passes

I walk
along a fence
in the back
talking
with someone
She is
older than me
but only
by a few years
She is thinking
about
the problems
of want and need
Questions
she asks me
to reflect
upon

A bright
light
fills in
the space
where she is
standing

Children
hold sticks
run around
We can hear
them yelling in the
background
The screens
fade
up
and out
I am
helping her
think
not with
thoughts of my own
more with hers

We find
a clearing and
turn
toward it
She
reaches for
my arm
Her hand
never
makes contact
Up ahead
in the distance

a line of trees
blur
The sound of
children's voices
muffle
In the fog
I am
whole
with no
boundaries

Under the bright sun
once cold
She clicks her
tongue
and turns
It won't go easy
a voice
we hear say
from outside
our heads

I bring
my left hand
to my
temple to
pause
collect myself
or make sense of
the voices

I hear while
her talking
keeps on
"proceeds"
I may say
as I nod
my head
while
touching
the left temple
with middle
finger
One of the
screens
sinks down
On the other
side
of the fence
a swimming pool
empty and covered
in leaves dirt
twigs and bugs

I motion
for help
The sun is
sinking
just
at the
horizon

She cannot
let me go
It is an
order
from somewhere
Some
one
I have to trust
Every
meadow
a blank side
over the passage
from above
the tilted
window
I turn
around
No one
is holding
the mirror
in front of
or behind
my self

A head
around the
center
falls down
the gaping
hole

From where
we have
arrived

And not gone

In a medieval village I write a poem called "Utterance." Peering out from behind a curtain. I'm thinking about the carnival, saturnalia, forces of power, animals and humans roaming a filthy marketplace, revolution.

It's November, 2014. My first book is going to print. The name I was given will appear on its cover. I have a feeling this name won't be mine for much longer. I am out in the streets over the police killings of Eric Garner, Michael Brown, Laquan McDonald, Tamir Rice. Trampling down Broadway, making noise outside the police station, avoiding being kettled in the street, running en masse onto the freeway.

The poem "Utterance" isn't there. It's barely me. It is distant—in another time and place.

Between 2009 to 2014—the years before, during, and after Occupy Oakland—my first book is composed. I'm reading all of Proust's *À la recherche du temps perdu*, watching every film by Rainer Werner Fassbinder, Apitchatpong Weerasethakul, Bela Tarr, reading *Capital vol. I*, reading *Dhalgren*.

At the end of 2011, I'm living in an apartment in downtown Oakland, five blocks from the encampment at Oscar Grant Plaza. Thumping helicopters day and night amplify the tensions in my body, a coursing energy that doesn't stop for weeks and months. My neighborhood becomes something else. In what was a sleepy downtown just a few years before, the center fills with people and energy. The city morphs and changes daily. It splits. An undercurrent that's always there rises to the surface, only to be violently stamped down. As long as it's active I don't get involved in the day-to-day organizing, but I show up to demos, participate in a few general assemblies, shut down the port, and walk through Laney College during J28 Move-In Day with a person playing a tuba, someone carrying a carrying a chair on their head, friends, poets, communists, anarchists, some people I don't like very much, and thousands of others.

At the beginning and end of *The Undying Present*, Quentin Compson stands on a bridge looking down into the water. He's going to jump. I'm standing there too, like a ghost embodying his ghostly body and writing from inside it. I gaze down and see mayflies skim on the surface of the water, as described by the writer who wrote it. I do all kinds of drag in the book. The "I" is not me. Also, it is all me.

In the end, the narrator lifts a book and reads what's there: the delicate fibers of a leaf in water waving slow as the motion of sleep, the pointed horror, the clean flame, mayflies skimming at the surface. Quentin looks up at me—a looking out, a looking back—from inside the book to the one whose hands hold it. Me to you, he might say, or me to you, I say. One text to the next that hasn't yet been written. Each stacks a section of the bridge together, from one land mass to another, building them as we go.

My apartment in downtown Oakland is in an old brick building on a tree-lined street. I move into it the summer of 2011 with Kate, my cat Sisa, and her dog Bear. Something like $1,350 a month for this spacious two-bedroom corner apartment on the third of three floors, with big windows and no shared walls. It's perfect. After spending one year in a coast-to-coast long-distance relationship, and another in a dark, mildly rancid apartment in Adams Point, we get cozy. We watch sports and movies, take the dog for walks at the lake, read and write, see friends. I have a committed reading practice, but I'm undisciplined with my writing. I learn from watching Kate write *Fault Tree*. I watch her run a marathon. I watch her take classes toward a nursing degree. She tries things out. I want to be a person who tries things out, but it feels impossible. I'm too anxious all the time. I am also eight years younger than Kate, so I tell myself it's something to strive for.

There's something else. Throughout our relationship Kate calls me Staiti, rarely Erika. When I let my hair grow out, she clasps it like a ponytail when I'm driving and says, "hiii Errrrika." It sounds so funny and we laugh. She sees this costume I wear. It's a joke between us. It doesn't feel bad. It's light. Since she's my partner, others follow suit, calling me Staiti too. It sticks. It is my name.

Kate leaves in 2013 and I drive with her halfway across the country, then fly back to the Bay Area as she carries on to Durham. I can afford to keep the apartment so I do. I let people stay in the spare room. First Marlo, then Trisha, then Jamie, then Sam. When I move out in 2017, I keep the apartment in my name and illegally sublease it to Jeanne and Joan, then Dia. Kate begrudgingly agrees to keep her name on the lease for all these years, lest the rent be raised to market value. I finally give up the apartment in 2020, hand over the keys on March 24, five days after California announces a mandatory statewide stay-at-home order due to COVID-19.

Now it's November, 2014, and Trisha crashes with me in the apartment. We barely know each other but she just moved from New York and needs a place to land. She's dating Kenower, my friend. I'm dating Maya, who I'm obsessed with and who loves me back—but not in that all-consuming way that I need because I'm insecure and miserable. Trisha's presence is energizing. She's young and sharp. I've heard about her from friends and poets and the internet. I have formed impressions before meeting her— mostly wrong, of course. She becomes a real person. I'm drawn in.

Having Trisha around motivates me to write again. I write a poem called "Utterance." With my first book about to be published, "Utterance" is the first poem that looks toward whatever the next book will be. I start reading Bakhtin's *Rabelais and His World*. I think using the carnival of the Middle Ages could be a way to write through whatever is happening with me and gender, still largely out of reach. The following year, "Utterance" becomes the last poem published under the name Erika Staiti.

Trisha moves out of my place and into a building in Temescal where Lindsey and Steve live. We remain friends. It's kinda flirty. A few months later, we start dating. She's still with Andrew, and I'm still with Maya, and we're seeing each other. This is my dream arrangement but something about the dynamic feels off. A month later, she and Andrew break up. I'm upset because it ruins the balance. A couple months later, Maya and I break up. I tell Trisha I like her a lot, and it's fun for now, but I don't think it's going to last very long.

Utterance

We've disrupted your gathering
group of birds pecking around in the dirt
walk through as they scatter
on the path toward and away from
townsfolk nodding at the carnival
bare feet over dry brittle grass
join the cattle, a herd of some
while the goatherd vies with the shepherd
for a valuable position on a banknote
the fool shall be
the first and in the end
an execution

In gossip circles, men decide things
they snarl at cylinders
spooking horticulture rings
cuckolds in the coop they are
chickening out
as they scatter amongst their own

What an inconvenience to be seen she thinks
and pulls a piece of hair from the eyes
but they are always looking
to state a case and I am often beating myself
with a spiked wand given to me by my mother
how often I am inconvenienced as well, she sighs

When the brakes engaged a lean gray horse spun around and fell /
the action was at half speed because we were watching from afar /
spindly trees crack apart in the woods / gears of carousel sabo-
taged by gophers teeth plunged into metal plates a shrieking chain
reaction outside the head / grubby hands clutch fake gold horns
/ standing behind and beside while bracing the small body that
sticks to itself / plastic bag filled with baby carrots falls into sludge

Hot in the room, oven running
puncture wounds deep in gut
no surface / mark / pound / hash / collision
it's swine if you want a taste

Army of jerks tramples through neighborhood
we are assessing the chances of an earthquake
causing major damage to the roof
it's categorically tragic, the farce

A startling sentiment dazzles
witches mown down around a maypole
hard against the rumble of quick machines
to the scattering of tools and howling
a sweet tune if you could remember it
witches concocted the accordion that heaves
without tone until its keys are pressed
the sound mesmerizes a gallery
of twits in mercurial whirlpool
swine, don't you come here

It's some kind of performance it is, all relations
eventually I come to like the days-long silence, she
says, rank formulations, while he talks and talks
and taps the desk with authority
the crunch of bones between teeth
crushing the bones to dust

A flower vase delicately perched on a mantle
I pour a glass of wine and hand it to you by the stem
scissors left on countertop
blood vessels against the edge of skin
a blade slides up and down his thigh

From the projector, light flickers against the eye.
Was it the image that did us wrong?

The barricade begins as a wall and ends as an enclosure / on the
outside which is inside out / I rest my tongue against the stone
and lick upward / against rough surface scraping tongue until
patch-marked scratches break the plane and beads emerge / black
shoe steps on swine a foot on that face / along wall of enclosure
and barricade licking it all / pink puffy face boot on the pink cheek
/ turn around and tearing apart / over the mark / scratches in the
dirt, earth, hellscape / contours of rough tongue bleeding / along
the arm, bleeding from the fingertips, the anus, the ear / bleeding from the centerpiece, the puncture wound, artificial heart /
bleeding a quotation, bleeding in memoriam, bleeding from where
there was already blood / the womb

A performance for one
is it real? is it worth it?
chaos lunges forward out of necessity
this trouble on the horizon
it's glaring
particles screaming things
without sound, just sentiment

The performance goes on and on
from a self, long ago, ages ago
misery of a relentless imaginary
you are prisoner to it

No, it chokes your nature out
of an absence or disappearance
you are so bewildered
so arbitrary and unimportant
a little convoluted

Only tyranny in view
the outer shell bears the marks
of work, displacement, failed pursuits
slathered in high octane fluid
as a drawn limb, a quartered limb
seeping from the mouth
lying under foot
oh, it is your boot
behind my ear
and there goes
another century

I have a pretty bad memory. I spend a lot of time thinking about it. If I had a good memory I would probably not think about it so much. I wonder what causes my bad memory. Trauma? Forgetfulness? A partner might correct me about my timeline. Or might say, we already talked about that, remember? I remember things in my own way, like the quality of light in a film, or the specks of truth at the core of a story instead of what happens on the surface of the narrative. I might read an entire book and have nothing to say except that it was good, because I felt it was good, I felt it, but I didn't think about what to say about it. I just let it move through me, trusting that some of its bright debris slipped into my system.

I've been writing in journals off and on for most of my life. Nothing spectacular, just narrating events of the day. I don't do this writing as if I'm a poet. I don't try. It's just me talking to myself. The journal writing has been useful for checking my memory. I scroll through a notebook from years ago and find myself confronted with a narrative I believed to be true—but there it is, written in my own hand, differently. Or I come across something that doesn't change my perception at all, doesn't hold real meaning—just a remnant of a previous iteration of myself. I'm reminded by notebooks that although I've grown and changed, and the world has too, my thoughts from over twenty years ago remain similar to the ones I hold now. Not the details, but the overarching concerns.

I start to think about what the next book could be. What if I came forward a little more, bared pieces of my life and experiences a little more explicitly. Why would anyone care about the details of my life? Everybody's got their own life to savor. Some might counter, why would anyone care about a kind of writing that obscures the details of your life? Readers are hungry for details of others' lives, driven by a kind of voyeurism that helps make their own life, and these times, more bearable. Some read others' lives because pieces of the story might resonate with their own, validating something they feel inside but haven't quite articulated, or that differ from their lives and so offer new ways of thinking. Some care less about lived lives and relish a text's structure, or shifts, or style. Others might simply let the text move through them, allowing themselves to be speckled by its debris.

In the year my book comes out, I write thirty pages of memories about the community park from my childhood for some reason. I try to map out the park in my mind, but there are just specks and mostly gaps. It's the occurrences that stand out, like when the lifeguards at the pool blow their whistles for everyone to get out because there's a turd in the water. Or at the playground, I'm on the seesaw with a kid I don't know. I can feel in my gut a distrust of him, but I don't know what distrust is, or what a gut is, as in, instinct, and whether I should trust mine. I'm afraid he will jump off the seesaw when I'm way up at the top and not ease me down, use his words to say, let's stop now, and level it so our feet touch the ground and we take turns getting off. Each up and down we go, he's smiling and I'm smiling because I want to appear like I'm having fun, but I feel fear. Then it happens. He hops off and I crash to the ground.

The memory wasn't written. Did it really happen? How could I know. I didn't tell my mother who was standing off to the side talking with another mother. Having few memories from childhood, I wonder why do I remember this? -Because it's preserved in my body. The impact as I hit the ground. And the lesson that I have something called instinct. And something else, something that lasts, something like shame.

Another one, more diffuse. I'm walking along the fence between the baseball field and the parking lot. The person next to me is a friend, but she's someone I don't meet until I'm twenty-six years old. She's older than me by twelve years and she's describing her dissertation as I listen. But I'm just a child. Have I combined two memories into one? Or is it a dream?

In 2015, I write a poem. I arrive on a hill. I call it "Stranded."

Some version of this memory sneaks into the poem. As aura, as background. The specificity of the memory or dream dissipates. It takes on the qualities of the poem, infuses itself into the poem, gives the poem something, and the poem gives it something back: a place to reside, in a different pitch.

After my book is published, I become more obsessed with names. I keep a long list that I add to and repeat and go back to and ask Alana and Marlo and Maya and Kate and Trisha what they think. I come up with new names and add them to the list and repeat the same names with different spellings and ask what they think again. Of course, there's more going on than just: *name*, but I channel all my gender anxiety into obsessing over my name.

In 2015, the local poetry scene I participate in confronts several incidents of sexual assault from the previous year. There are meetings and emails and pain and betrayal and the splintering of friendships. The same year, two people who are considered powerful in the national scene of poets I participate in are called out for racist acts. Social media ramps to a fever pitch. The same year, Walter Scott and Freddie Gray are killed by cops, Sandra Bland is found dead in a jail cell, Caitlyn Jenner comes out as trans, civil lawsuits stack up against Bill Cosby, nine people are killed in a targeted gun assault on the first African Methodist Episcopal Church in Charleston, Donald Trump announces his campaign to be president.

Throughout this year and the next, I spend countless hours slumped on the couch watching YouTube videos of twenty-year-olds who've started hormones or gotten top surgery. I'm in my thirties, and it feels impossible, like I can't do it, but I also can't keep living like this. I'm standing in my own way and the more I become aware of it, the worse I feel. I have trans friends, Jaime for nearly twenty years, but I don't talk to him or anyone else about what I'm going through. I'm afraid they'll all think I'm making it up. I can't imagine saying I've suddenly realized that I'm trans too. Really. After all this time? Come on.

I write an untitled poem—a third piece of writing after "Utterance" and "Stranded" that asserts itself as part of the next book. I think I can use it as a framework for the book, like a short exercise in what I want the book to do. It doesn't end up being anything like the book, I don't think, but it's included in it.

In this poem, I'm not standing on the bridge looking down into the water as Quentin did. Instead, I'm in the depths of the water—a tadpole born into a murky swamp surrounded by flames. The poem feels messy. I can't help but be breathless and intense when I read it aloud at a couple of readings. My voice shakes and gets faster toward the end. My hands tremble when I hold the printed papers in front of me at the microphone. I'm a boy in a fairytale, a filthy, messy boy. I'm at the carnival. I don't know what it is. The parents are figures for something else. I'm trying things on. Something in there is me

[Untitled]

In the holding place that spawned me
amid the pointing and the horror
I was a tadpole trapped in your marsh
walled by surrounding flames

My belly slides over algae covered stones
here in the marsh, swampland
the muddy womb I spring from—

A tadpole, my feet are not yet formed
tail moves like a motor
I'll stick with the horror as long as I'm here
yes I am worthy of death at your hands mother
your desire to destroy me is real
as my little tail propels me through these fires I can't see
what you create and undo with your hands this world, what hell
will you bring us now

My sticky eyelids open and I see nothing
this isn't what we planned
it's not what I wanted either
I warned you and you didn't listen you never listen—

My little white legs step out of the tub as I reach for the towel
I was that monster on the couch behind you
no it was your father eating an apple there
my father he was lying on the couch

holding an apple, bringing it to his mouth, taking a bite
and staring at us while crunching apple bits between his teeth,
menacing father teeth
and you, you were in front of him
he was on the couch and you were lying down
I watched you I watched you lay yourself down, down on the
ground before him
but it wasn't my father, it was an older, male poet, he had warm
eyes and a gentle touch, he was a quiet beast

Under what conditions would you demand a stable subject
to emerge from the swamp, slimy and terrible
to look on you with its beady eyes
and say yes, what I am about to tell you
is real. I am a subject. stable. someone you can trust. you will hear
me and you will bring up the flames. you will ignite the wall of
flame and you will see yourself as a stable subject. you will dis-
solve the subject and take it into your mouth, grinding it down
with your teeth.

I was at the carnival, standing alone behind the Ferris wheel, waiting for you to arrive. you knew what I wanted to do when you got
there. you would be wet and ready for me. but you would never
come because in that moment you were drowning in the lake. if
it was me who threw you in, I am very sorry. I cannot have you
existing away from me, that's all. do you understand? yes, I think
so. no, I don't think you do.

Every time you walk away, turn the corner, you cease to exist.
you die, you die to me, are dead to me, every time you turn, you

die. but every time I turn from you, I get bigger. what happens to you when I turn? do you want to kill me, do you think I'm dead, do you wish for my death, this is a real question and I forbid you from answering it.

After I turn the corner, not only are you out of reach, I no longer know where I am myself, you see, not a stable subject, not even a subject at all. the problem isn't that I don't have a mother. it is that I do, and when you turn the corner the gaping hole that is my mother grows inside me. it expands and multiplies. my body is a patch of holes and they grow bigger and the threads that hold the holes together are fraying. I ask you to sew me up but instead you take the needle and drive it into my left eye and then into my right. now I have a body of holes and two bleeding eyes gouged by my own hand. it's true, you did it, but I gave you the tools. you only did what you were supposed to. your role is very clear here.

and mine too, though nothing is stable.

In the mansion I was a boy a dirty little boy wearing suspenders and expensive clothing with snot on my face and parents who were so filthy and rich that I couldn't be any subject but "boy" and "dirty" like, in the head. they were hosting a dinner party at the house. the guests were all these aristocratic types. the house-maids, cook, and butler were in the back room. there was a snake under the table but only I could see it. I was sitting at the table with my legs swinging, not long enough to reach the floor, and I picked at the food with my little dirty fingers. mother was mildly embarrassed and father paid me no mind at all. he was reading passages out of a big old dusty book, maybe it was a bible or a dictionary. I couldn't make sense of the conversations. the guests became empty figures of nothingness, like air, air with shapes, sitting around, saying nothing, snorting their own words and air.

I was sitting at the dinner table pulling on myself under the tablecloth while the maid was in the kitchen waiting for me to come in. instead, I walked around the table filling everyone's wine glass, because father asked me to because father asked me to. one day I will say no to father, one day I will walk into the kitchen, join the others, and burn down the estate. I picture this in my head as I fill the wine glasses, then I walk out of the dining room into the parlor and I walk to the corner of the parlor and I begin to pee, I pee in the corner of the parlor, that's what I do, I stand there peeing all over the expensive Persian fucking rug. then I go back to the dining room and take my seat at the table and pee under the table as I eat, as they drink up their wine, peeing with a smile. I look over to the other side of the table and see my mother sucking on her thumb.

This didn't happen, so what happened? I went into mother's bedroom and lay on the bed, waited for her to come in and—because she was you, my lover, my mistress, my mentor, my professor, my boss, my wife. she entered the bedroom holding a package in her hands and it was from her husband, my father and he wasn't lying on the couch eating an apple then. not anymore. no apples for daddy.

Earlier, during dinner, a storm raged outside and I thought it might clatter the shades into the window and maybe even smash the window in, but I couldn't find the line, I guess I deleted it and saved over the old version, because it's gone, the storm, like it never happened.

If I wanted to hold onto what you say to me, I'd need a memory for it, but my memory is comprised of instances of shame sewn up all together. so when you reach for me with sweetness, will I store the moment or will it move right through me and disappear like a dream I can't grab on to—

Because in the end I was right. you turned the corner and everything died, the story collapsed on itself. The carnival booths rotted into the ground, the lake dried up, and the servants burned down their quarters, along with the rest of the house. The swamp was still there waiting for us to return to it—the stable subject and the not-even-a-subject—and there were the frayed pieces of thread, dangling from my holes, as you grab onto them in an attempt to get past the walls of flame that surround the marsh that is you, that you were spawned into, amid the horror of all of our days, our creation.

Seldom walks beside me. His hands are bunched in his pockets. Eyes down at the ground. He kicks a piece of glass.

My hands are in my pockets too. My left hand holds a stone. I turn it around in the pocket, hold the stone tight.

We're not talking much. We walk at a relaxed pace.

The road goes uphill, then downhill. We pass a shopping center, we pass tents under a freeway overpass, we pass a bar, we arrive at an art school.

Seldom and I walk into the art school and down the long white hallway. My right hand curls around the phone in my pocket. I take the hand out, look at the phone, put it back in.

We walk out the back door of the building into the street.

A ragged street, a cart overturned, a pile of soiled clothes, the wind whips and stops. Sun rays crashing down at an angle.

The conversation is about to get underway—
But you lost it, didn't you

When I was a child I was ushered into a body of water that was surrounded by fire, this is what they told me, the beings that tell stories as we sleep.

The old wooden apartment I rented with a friend, bringing someone through, running into the old landlady, having something else
to do, getting back late or having to leave early—

It was a duplex I moved into with a friend, it was 2001, the landlady almost didn't rent to us. one dyke and one trans guy, or two
dykes, or two trans guys. whatever she saw, she was tentative
about renting to us.
maybe it was because we were young and had no prior rental
history
there's always a reason behind the reasons, one or many reasons
maybe she was dealing with health problems, it could be anything
the question still rumbles in the background.

But we did move in. it was the Clinton Street pocket of southeast
Portland near the theater, the video store, and Dots. never met
the neighbors till one day they rang our doorbell with a note in
their hand. it was a note someone had written to me. the neighbors were worried and asked if I was okay. they knew something I
didn't want to. that I was in danger.

What do you do—

We walk back through the building, out the front doors, looking
for the car. Seldom didn't drive me here. We walked together from
the train station but he will drive himself back alone. I'm going
home to someone else.

I don't see him again until many years later.

I'm moving out of my apartment in downtown Oakland into a house with my partner in South Berkeley. I come across boxes of papers and journals, stop packing to read through old stuff.

I find an old poem. It involves a narrator walking home from work to find a man sitting naked in the tub with a glass of wine in his hand, talking about things like "Art" and "Hierarchy." His name is Libel. The narrator enters the bathroom and asks Libel to leave, but he ignores them and keeps talking. The narrator sits on the top of the toilet seat with their head in their hands. At the time of writing it, I only show the poem to a few people. Nobody likes his name, Libel. Nobody likes the poem at all. They say they don't get it. I don't get it much either. It ends up in a box.

The narrator—who I later name Hue—is a she at the time of writing it, a they when I find the box of stuff while packing, and is now a he. In other words, the narrator is me.

When I reread the poem, sitting on the floor in my living room surrounded by boxes, it's 2017, ten years after I wrote it. I've just started hormones. I'm surprised to see the line "Libel, that's my penis you're holding." I try to imagine myself in 2007 writing these words. What did I mean? I slide my consciousness back into the self of that time to see if there's anything I can grasp of it, but nothing's there. Just me making a joke. It sounds funny, I think that I thought.

So what happens: I'm sitting in my half-packed apartment reading the poem, thinking how Hue and Libel have been trapped all these years—Libel in the Tub, Hue on the Toilet—in this poem in the box. I need to release them, set them free. I try writing new poems to reposition the characters elsewhere, but it doesn't work. I go away on writing retreat and call on Seldom to help. And there we are, Seldom and me, walking side by side at the beginning of a new poem. I'm trying to explain it all to him but I don't know how.

I think we need to blow it up. The poem? What if you try to save it. *I've been trying, it's taking a toll. I think we need to blow up the poem and hope they escape the ruins.* No more time in the tub and on the toilet. The building in the city of my writing that was half-erected, then ignored. I hope I can escape the ruins of the parts of poems I've been holding onto closed in a box.

Seldom needs a team so we call on Venn and Chase to help. Samuel will be there too.

I pick up Seldom and the others from the airport. We move at seventy-five miles per hour on the freeway, over a bridge, veer right for the exit, loop around to another freeway, merge, then hang right to get off, up the four-lane street, through the center of the city and turn. We arrive at the place where they'll stay for the duration of the experiment.

We pull up in front of an old building and get out of the car. The saturation drains out, colors slide off the screen and down, like a stream from a bucket of water poured off the curb by the owner of a market wearing a white apron who looks up and down the street before turning to go back into his shop. The colors slink off the frame, a stream coursing through the streets behind us.

I swing open the front door of the building and hold it for them. I say, "all the way up," and carry their bags as we climb the old spiral staircase. I've got one bag hanging from my shoulders, one slung to the side, and one in each hand, as we reach the top floor and I set the bags down to pull a rusty key out of my pocket

"and planted their bones"
I once wrote

I jiggle the key and we enter the apartment. They look around.

The construction is a mess, walls falling apart in unused rooms. I've done this before, I think, in that building from the first book. There, I was a figment of a person wherein my reflection was a ghostly woman running in a dress through fields, a double image of myself I couldn't access. Now I'm walking along a road next to Seldom, who doesn't hold my hand. We would've held hands on the walk. In my memory we did.

"I would like for you to destroy it."
His steps slow. I adjust to match his pace. He stops.

Looking out into the urban wilderness. Overgrown weeds take over the median. A mattress leans against the side of an electric pole, sinking toward the street on both ends. A truck barrels past. I look to the sky. He doesn't respond.

You decide what to do. I can't anymore. I'm done.
He says okay and gets in the car. I walk to the BART station.

Back in the apartment, the walls of the interior are a dirty yellow.
Curtains, and the way he draws them closed as everyone settles in.

I'm standing in the middle of the room with a thought. It's like
a bubble blown on the end of a plastic ring. When he enters the
room, it pops. *I lost it,* I say. It was still too wet. Like the dream
you had and left forgotten.

It starts with a poem, he says in the room. Everyone listens as
he opens the narration. It begins with destruction and ends with
beginning—

I leave them to sort things out. I am not here to determine the
actions, dialogue, or outcome.

I climb into the fireplace, put my hands against the cold humid
walls of the cave, crawl through for about an hour, and emerge on
a cliff above the ocean.

From the cliff I walk down a path to the lower ridge, pass an abandoned house in a junk-filled landscape down to the ocean. I sit on
the sand and rest my arms around the tops of my knees. I hold
small rocks in my hands as I watch the sea approach and recede. I
lie back, weaving my fingers together behind my head. My elbows
don't lie flat on the ground—they hover above it. This is because
I didn't raise my arms for months after top surgery to avoid pulling on the incisions and stretching the scars, so I lost a range of

mobility. I don't mind. Still it's relaxing, to have the sun on my face, to feel my breathing steady.

After some time, I sit up. Two people and a dog walk past. There are huge rocks way out in the distant water. I stare for a long time at the contrast between the colors of the sky, the varying shades of blue in the water, and the edge of white foam. The sky looks almost purple, I think, the colors are so rich. Then I remember I'm wearing tinted sunglasses. I take them off and everything dulls. I put them back on.

I pull out my phone and record the sounds of the ocean. I think that someday I might want to use the recording in a film, even though I dislike the constant impulse to grab at everything I experience: photos, video, audio, writing things down. I materialize present moments so I can revisit them in future present moments, to make use of them somehow, in a piece of art, or as a way to track my progress in this life.

At the end of 2015, I send an email to friends, poets, and select family members announcing I've changed my name and pronoun. I think this will solve the problem. Instead, I feel worse than before. I made something known that's been hiding a long time, that I myself did not want to see. The act of stating my new name does not feel emancipatory. I remain crouched inside myself for another year. Nobody notices because I'm a master performer. A friendship that I hold a little too tightly shatters in my hands. I feel rejected and devastated. I think this is all I can say about 2016, the year after I change my name and pronoun, and the year before I start taking hormones.

I go for a hike with Ari at Strawberry Canyon. It's the time of year when milky oat tops are harvestable. He pulls a plastic bag out of his backpack and we run our hands up the stem collecting hand-fuls and shoving them into the plastic bag. Ari points to things on our walk. That's elderberry, that's nettle. I follow him on a narrow path off the main trail. He climbs over a fallen tree and then I do. We go further until we reach a clearing. He says, in a joking way, this is where you can bring your Grindr hookups, and I laugh. I don't mention that I had the same thought. Ari and I sit side by side on a fallen tree. We are less than six feet apart and not wear-ing masks. Reckless pandemic behavior, but he's fully vaccinated and I'm one shot in. I tell him I'm struggling to write about 2016, that it's all a fog, that nothing happened, that I was sitting in a holding pattern, unable to do anything. He says, but something *was* happening, even if you felt stuck at the time, because you got out of it.

In 2016, I do enroll in a Wild Goose Qigong class. The class is eight weeks long and when it's over I take it again and again. I keep taking the class for a year until I've learned the Dayan Qigong form—the first 64 movements—well enough that I can practice on my own. In class, I say my name is Syd but I don't assert a pronoun, so they call me she. It's here that I become aware that my shoulders are always tight. My teacher points it out constantly. It becomes almost a joke in the class. The repetition forces me to begin drawing my own awareness to the tightness of my shoulders. I find myself catching it and then loosening on my own. Five years later, I still catch and loosen. Just did, actually, as I typed the last line.

I learn Dayan Qigong was developed in the Jin Dynasty (266-420 AD) by Daoist monks in the Kunlun Mountains. The monks use Chinese medicine principles, spiritual meditation, and the movements of the wild geese living among them to build a system of healing. For centuries, the practice is passed down from a grandmaster to a single apprentice in secret. I question my teacher on this point because it's so hard to believe. In any given moment, for seventeen hundred years, only one person and one apprentice at any point in time knew and practiced this form? My teacher says yes. I wonder how it comes to be that I learn it all the way over here. She occasionally mentions her teacher who she still practices with, Master Hui Liu, who is in her 80s. I'm intrigued so I research the rest on my own.

In 1908, at the age of thirteen, Yang Meijun was chosen as the twenty-seventh inheritor of Dayan Qigong by her grandfather, who then held the lineage. He tells her she cannot tell anyone, and she can't begin teaching it to another until she reaches the age of seventy. In 1978, when she turns seventy years old, she decides to share Dayan Qigong with not just one, but many, ending the secretiveness of centuries. She holds classes and teaches numerous apprentices, encouraging them to teach others. One of her hand-picked proteges is Master Hui Liu Ju, who, with her husband, opens the Wen Wu School of Martial Arts in El Cerrito, CA in 1973. Master Hui Liu travels back to China to study for many years with Grandmaster Yang Meijun, then brings the teachings to the Wen Wu School in the Bay Area, including to Maureen, who then teaches it to me.

At an open house at the Wen Wu School, I meet Grandmaster Hui Liu. She leads the group in a standing meditation. At the end, we all bow together. As my waist is bent, I hear her soft, accented, octogenarian voice roll over me: "we bow to the sky, to the earth, and to the teacher." At home, when I bow at the end of my practice, I pay respects to my teacher Maureen, to Master Hui Liu, and to Grandmaster Yang Meijun, tracing time over a century. In this bow, I also connect laterally to all those who practice Dayan Qigong—past, present, and future—who themselves, either knowingly or unknowingly, bow to Yang Meijun, inheritor of the ancient tradition, who released it to the world.

You know what else happens in 2016? I read a lot.

Not the usual stuff. I borrow a book about prehistoric Egypt from my boss at work, who's an Egyptologist, and learn about the Badarian and Naqada Cultures. It spurs me to read more about this era, between 4500–2000 BCE. I read about the Sumerians in Mesopotamia. I read about Harappa and Mohenjo-daro in the Indus Valley. I go back even further and read about the Natufian culture in Palestine, over thirteen thousand years ago. I am primarily interested in the Neolithic Revolution and the centuries preceding it. It's a transition that lasts for millennia. I want to learn about this turn, as I am, in this moment, an individual experiencing a gradual (glacial, it feels) turn of my own.

There is no single narrative of the global Neolithic Revolution. Each region undergoes its own transition, its own series of evolutions and revolutions. Settlements form and disappear, trade and merge. I read about how writing evolves and its relation to currency. Marks are made on envelopes to identify what tokens lie inside. Changes in agricultural practices and the domestication of animals lead to the development of sedentary communities, and then, to the rise of the state. Public buildings, taxes and administration, larger workforces, social stratification. The books I read are decades old, in a contentious field that is always changing. I don't take everything I read as received truth knowing archaeology, anthropology, and history, in general, have been fields primarily written by white colonizers. I'm curious about the most current discourse, which I know has complicated this perspective, but I don't explore it just yet. I'm only using the ideas as a loose framework anyway, as a conduit for my thinking and writing at this time.

I can't make sense of my own rhythms and systems, my own evolutions and revolutions, so I zoom out to a larger frame to fixate on this massive historical context. Then I zoom in to learn about specific cultures from different regions and eras. I am driven by curiosity, a desire to learn, and a kind of voyeurism that helps make my own life more bearable. How else to endure the brutality of these times?

At the end of 2016, I am invited to read at the Sponge reading series in West Oakland. I have nothing to read because I haven't been writing. I've been practicing qigong, reading about some of the first human settlements, and crouching inside myself. I decide to write something new for the reading at the last minute, which is something I did once before, back in 2009 for a reading at the Canessa Gallery in San Francisco. The scene of poets was so different then. I was so different. How to approach a similar strategy now?

But it doesn't matter because one week before the reading, a fire burns at a Ghost Ship warehouse party in Oakland and thirty-six people die. I write something specifically for the reading but it's different from what I originally thought I would write. How could it not be? When I read, people are crying. I am too. I wonder if it's fucked up that I did this.

Today is Wednesday. It's two days ago. I sit here writing at "Fresh and Best II" on Alice Street in downtown Oakland. What I write today I'll read on Friday, tonight, at the sponge reading in West Oakland. While I can't know tonight since I'm not there yet, I don't really know today either, even as it's happening, and it's hard to know anything about the Friday that just passed. All I know, here on Wednesday, is there's something on either side.

I've been having a lot of feelings. When I have a lot of feelings I shut people out, most especially those closest to me. I'm trying not to do this but it's hard. I don't want to write about how fucked up the world feels. It's always fucked. These peak moments feel like they're hitting harder, faster, more frequently. The more they try to destroy us the stronger we become, people say. It's not untrue. But in this world, we're never fully alive in the first place—always already damaged, and then we die. The ways we make ourselves glimmer in this half-death is what we see and love in each other, and the thing we most mourn when it's gone.

I was planning to write something new for this reading but then a wall rose up that divided last Friday with today. Ghost Ship. Now I feel grief and everyone around me feels grief, the entire city seems to be grieving. I tune into a local radio station on the way to work and they're talking about it, grief. My coworkers don't seem to feel grief but then they learn that they know someone who lost a son, so then they feel grief. Now it is Wednesday today, and between last Friday's fire and next Friday's reading—tonight—time stops holding any meaning, but something still gets tracked. It is change that's the real marker of time.

As I sit here trying to write about anything other than grief, I remember another time where I was scrambling to write before a reading. It was about eight years ago. I ended up writing something that sort of makes me cringe now, feels outdated and strange to me, as this surely will later on. The reading was about an orgy but it wasn't really about an orgy. It was more about poets and how they were relating to each other. It was about my perception of the local scene of poets in 2008.

The reading I gave was on January 17, 2009. After looking up the date of the reading I realize it took place just two weeks after Oscar Grant was killed by a cop in the Fruitvale BART Station. Things felt explosive then. The Israeli military campaign "Operation Cast Lead" was going on in Gaza. Israel ceased fire on January 18, after 1,440 Palestinian casualties, just thirteen on the Israeli side. Whatever little dramas I felt at this time inside me and in relation to my little scene of poet friends, there were large scale crises erupting in the city where I lived and also around the world.

Later that year, the fall of 2009, students at UC Berkeley, Santa Cruz, Davis, occupied buildings to resist tuition hikes. Friends dragged off and jailed. Court dates, pepper spray, building occupations. Wheeler Hall occupied—it was incredible—I hadn't seen anything like it. The UC actions lay some of the groundwork for the Occupy movement to grow as strong as it did in the Bay Area a couple of years later. Connections made between people, networks that could be built upon at a larger scale. Of course, divisions formed, too, just as much as alliances were made.

The death of Oscar Grant, a young Black man shot in the back while lying face down on the train platform—one murder in a centuries-long continuum of violence against Blackness—was all over the media. The protests at the time marked the beginning of a political turn for me, as I was back out in the streets again for the first time since the 2003 anti-war protests when I lived in Portland, Oregon. Once in the streets, I recalled all the times I had been before. When I spit on a cop in downtown Portland during a rally and my partner and I got in a fight because my partner believed the cop was there in a respectable capacity. How I screamed and ran and charged with the masses of people, how I lost my partner and didn't care. Enraged and impassioned, I felt like an animal. Again, in Oakland, it's familiar and new all at once. This time no spitting, same fury. The wall of dormancy, six years long, disintegrates, and in the years since, the number of times back out into the streets. I bring all the other times with me, hold them close, despite the walls between.

I look back at the reading from 2009. It's strange, the ways I thought about poets and myself in a time that feels so different, the other side of a wall. That night I read with Dodie Bellamy and Suzanne Stein at the Canessa Gallery in North Beach. We were invited by erica lewis, who was the guest curator for Colleen Lookingbill, a San Francisco poet who passed away in 2014 from cancer at the age of sixty-three. As a young earnest poet, it felt daunting to be reading with Dodie and Suzanne, two writers I highly respect, whose work has influenced and continues to inspire me. The reading was taking place in a period of heightened sociality in my scene of poets. I was relatively new to it all. Everything felt exciting and totally filled with stakes.

At the time, I was obsessed with micro-aspects of poets, everything I saw that I thought was wrong with them. It was like a politics for me. It was one of my loops. It seemed to me there was rarely ever any discord between the poets in my scene, not outwardly, not publicly. Everyone was friends because everyone was poets, and everything was all good. I wasn't so sure. I felt a lot of unspoken aggression bubbling up in different ways, shit rising up, everyone pushing it back down. I wanted ideological differences to come to the surface—aesthetics, politics—I wanted to argue about these things and to form friendships and allegiances around them. I wanted people to want this too. I admit, I don't think I made much of an effort to create or foster this myself, it was just something I wanted *them* to do, and something I could criticize them about not doing. Maybe what I wanted ended up happening, in a messy sort of way. Some version of it. I'm not sure.

All the breaks, shifting plates, our reconfigured selves.

When that man walked into the Pulse club in Orlando earlier this year and killed forty-nine gay Latinx people, I felt a particular kind of devastation that I couldn't understand right away. I was thinking about how grief is not only the present cause of the grief, but a recollection of all the previous times you've grieved. Each moment of grief holds within it all of them. So when yet another friend commits suicide, you not only miss that friend, you also miss the other friends you lost the same way. It stays with you.

Each time holds all the other times.

The Pulse shooting brought up feelings of every aggression and microaggression I had suffered or witnessed or heard about as a queer and trans person. I wasn't reliving specific instances so much as an overall feeling of being totally gutted out. I was surprised to be so impacted by the death of strangers. It took a while to register what was happening until I talked with Ariel and learned that they were feeling the same way too. It wasn't intellectual or empathetic, in the ways that we were seeing online—it was bodily, held in our cells and in the psyche. We were reliving our own moments of death, all the little deaths we suffer while living, the stares and comments, moments of invisibility, acts or threats of violence—the walls between one body and another, one humiliation or attack and another, one catastrophe and another, one decade and another, all melded together.

Memory, when it's visceral, felt in the body. It happens—that collapse of time.

[Breathe]

So when a fire breaks out in a warehouse a few days ago and dozens of people you know and don't know, friends, acquaintances, folks you've seen around at shows and parties, folks your friends know and love, people in your families, workplaces, social media networks, you feel the devastation inside your body and you feel it in the bodies of those around you. And then it hits you—you've been gutted again.

The gutting keeps going, even after death they keep gutting, they are already out to gut the rest of the warehouses in town. They're gutting with their grants and loans for already-established artists, wealthy tech influx gutting the rest, rampant houselessness, violence of the carceral state, the surveillance state, the militarized state, the fascist state, the murdering of Black people at the hands of police, lack of resources for mental health and disability needs, the high rate of suicide among trans people, refusal to rematriate land back to the Indigenous, the widening gap between the richest and everyone else, the detention and deportation of immigrants, separation of children from their families, climate change, the destruction of the land and its living beings for the sake of the perpetuation of this death machine in the name of profit, for the sake of a stability that has never been there, for the preservation of power—white supremacy and capitalism, hand-in-hand— power breeds conditions which allow it to gain more power. The new ways we've fallen into believing we're side-stepping such power, or going up against it, only to find we're playing into the new hand it dealt behind our back. The gutting continues as we make strides and take losses, over and over.

But I don't want to talk about these things right now, though I think about them a lot. *I want to know what devastation feels like in your body.* What do you know about it this time that you didn't last? What will you do with it next time?

I'm in a loop. I'm in many. Some are my own and some are others. We're all in our own individual loops concentrically connected to each other's loops, all within one immense grand loop. I want to break the fuck out, but the loops are all interconnected. You can't break one, not even a few, or a million. It's not the loops to break, not the walls, but the conditions that make them possible in the first place. And all the stuff that needs to break that's not material too—the rancid stuff in our minds. When the forces that control these conditions are destroyed, what awaits us on the other side? Who do we become over there? Are we ready?

Lately it's been hard to be present in this world so I spend time reading about the earliest civilizations. Egypt, Mesopotamia, 4,000 years ago, they were just beginning to develop written language. In Mesopotamia they used clay, so the Sumerian script, cuneiform, is scripted like wedge-shaped marks, impressed into clay. While in Egypt, hieroglyphics is a script that, while originally modeled in plaster, was refined with the use of reed pen to papyrus. The scripts were styled by the implement and surface used to write them. The medium structured the form.

During the 4th millennium, in Egypt and Mesopotamia, Palestine and Syria, city-states and pastoral communities were disappearing and emerging, trading with each other, asserting force over one another, slowly turning toward something new. The turn was agriculture. The process of farming and domestication of animals brought about the need for counting and written language, leading to accumulation of wealth and social stratification, power, gendered division of labor, property—all things recognizable to us under capitalism today. But not capitalism then, something else.

History is roughly marked by the invention of written language. The period before that is known as pre-history. The entirety of history then—all of civilization as we know it—is only ten percent of human life on earth. For two million years before that, humans and our predecessors were hunter-gatherers. This huge catastrophic wall of civilization we're living in—the entire loop of it—is tiny, and ninety percent of human existence took place on the other side.

I had to build this wall of history for myself. Not because the devastations get any easier, moments in the streets pushing against power, the social dynamics of a scene, mourning and grieving friends, strangers, oneself, all those little deaths daily. But because the entire frame of it—the mold that was beginning to set 4,000 years ago, that has defined the scripts we now follow—there was something on the other side of history back there, and there's something else ahead.

We are in the middle. Today is Wednesday. I don't know.

Timestamp: Saturday, January 17, 2009
Location: Canessa Gallery, San Francisco

Go, Poet. Go!

For months I was trying to top the orgy but I couldn't. There was no way I could top the orgy. It was too big and powerful. Too many people owned the story of the orgy. I had to let the orgy top me.

My hope was to try to speak my version of the orgy, my story, but as hard as I tried I couldn't speak it because my mouth was stuffed full of shit and the orgy was shoving more shit into my mouth and the shit was dripping down my throat and collecting in my belly. The orgy tied me up and humiliated me and threw me on the ground and fucked me hard.

That was the story I wrote. I was going to read that story tonight but I decided not to. I know where I stand with the orgy. I know how the orgy feels about me. The orgy is a powerful thing. It's still here almost a year later. The orgy did things to the people in it, changed them. Some of the people decided to retreat and be more careful where they put their hands and tongues. Some people yawned and carried on their lives but were less interested in coming to events where the others would be. Some people became more excited and eager and aggressive with their sexuality. And others continued to be the way they have always been except that they decided it was time to stop feeling guilt and shame, because no matter how many orgies, or how many people out there know about the orgies and talk about the orgies, orgies were going to continue to be a part of this person's life and there was nothing this person could do to prevent their involvement in them, unless this person repressed parts of their being which they were not willing to do, and in dealing with months and months of feeling shame and guilt and cringing inside from their actions they finally decided it was enough. The shame and guilt had to stop. That one is me.

I am hard. I am so fucking hard and tough. I only want you to want me. Don't love me. OK? It would be a disaster. It's not that I want to be hard, I just don't have any other way. I hope you understand.

I am hard, but I'm also very sensitive. I have many feelings. As much as I don't want anyone to love me I also very desperately want everyone to love me. I can't stand the thought of people not loving me. Love me, but don't get too close.

I wrote about other things in the story I was going to read tonight. I wrote about other things besides the orgy fucking me. I wrote about poets, about Bay Area poets. I mean about the Bay Area poets that I see all the time at readings. I am critical of the poets. It is because I love the poets that I am critical of them. In the story I'm not going to read tonight, I wrote about how all the poets walk around with their mouths stuffed full of shit. And when the shit gets too heavy they spit the shit out onto the walls. I wrote about how every wall of every reading is covered in shit. And when readings are over, all of the poets, with globs of shit stuffed in their mouths, dripping down their throats and collecting in their bellies, they say the reading was good. The reading was good huh? Yeah the reading was good. How good was that reading? Dude that reading was good. Hey that was a good reading. Yeah good reading. Yeah that reading was good. The reader says thanks. Then the poets say who's going to the bar. Are you going to the bar? Is anyone going to the bar tonight? Let's go to the bar. I'll buy you a drink if you come to the bar. Are you coming? Cool, see you at the bar.

I wanted to talk about the poets and how they aren't very friendly to anyone who is not them, including other poets. I wanted to talk about how the poets don't allow anyone else to see them. When anyone brings a non-poet to a reading it is torture, for everyone. I will never meet anyone new if I keep hanging out with the poets. Nobody new ever comes around. I wish at every reading, every poet brought one friend who was not a poet. If that happened, I wish the poets would be nice to the non-poets. I wish the poets would realize that they could learn from the non-poets, that it's nice to be friends with non-poets. That maybe non-poets are good for poets, in the long run. It is not that the poets are mean, it is just that they're scared. They are scared and they must protect themselves. I understand this because it is how I am with love. I am scared. I must protect myself. Nobody get too close.

It's not that the poets don't like people, they just need people to insist their way into the group. To do this, all you've gotta do is go to every reading and allow yourself to be ignored at every reading for like a year or more, and then eventually something gives, and the poets decide you're okay. In allowing yourself to be ignored for over a year, and continuing to go to the readings, you proved to the poets that you are "committed" to poetry, that you are worth talking to, and being taken seriously. I am talking about my experience here, or my perception of my experience. Now the poets have absorbed me and I have allowed myself to be absorbed by them. Now I absorb others. I love the poets, I really do. But I also worry about the poets. I also worry about myself.

My biggest problem with falling in love is that I lose myself. I let the love absorb me. I give myself up to the love and the love controls me. This is why I have not allowed myself to love or be loved in the past few years. But in the past few years, I have given myself up to the poets. Have I replaced love with the poets? Maybe this is why I so badly want to make out with so many of the poets. I'm asking them to fill a space they shouldn't fill, a space that, even if they wanted to take it, they are not cut out for. Making out with the poets is a problem. It has to stop. I mean there are a few poets I would like to make out with sweet and tender and behind closed doors—even though that would be impossible because I would want it to be a secret, because secrets are sexy, but the poets don't know from secrets, and the poets often don't know from sexy either.

Well, I've had enough of the drunk sloppy cluster-fucks. They are so un-sexy, so messy. It's already messy enough in here. If the poets keep making out with each other, the community will implode. Maybe we could use a good implosion. Let it all shake out, settle down, start from scratch, pick up on a new track. Hello? Bay Area? Is something very wrong in here? Or we can close our eyes and keep kissing, or we can close our eyes and keep talking

about the kissing, whichever it is that you do. It will all shake itself
out, with or without you, anyway.

As soon as I proved that I was committed to poetry, I never had
to talk about poetry again. I could talk about poets. I could talk
about making out. I could say things like, the reading was good,
yeah the reading was good, who's going to the bar? I used to be
able to talk about poetry. Now I am lazy and incapable of it. I hate
how many times I've used the word poetry and poets and community in this. Everything I'm saying is wrong. I hope you disagree
with me and prove me wrong. I hope this talk is more messy than
the community. If the community is more messy than this talk,
the community is fucked. It's about practice. It's about integrity.
It's about insecurity. It's about Gaza. Why haven't I said anything
about Gaza. But how could I possibly say anything about Gaza.
Where is my place to say something about Gaza? What is my duty
as a poet? To say, to leave unsaid? Or is my place to say: I can't
help but speak even if I know that my speech is futile. I believe my
duty is to say, how dare I. Either way. Everything is despicable.

Everybody walks around with shit stuffed in their mouths. The
shit clogs their throat and collects in their bellies. Everybody spits
the shit out when it gets too heavy.

There's something else, many other things. More than the making
out. Something about the making out is wrong, but it happens.
It happens and it keeps happening and who the fuck cares.
Something about it feels right even though it feels wrong. There is
something still about implosion. And something about the people
who do not partake in the making out but who are invested in the

fact that it happens. Something about that vicariousness, something about the distraction.

Something about the fact that things are being left unsaid.

Hello. Hello. Do you like my hat? I do not. Goodbye. Goodbye.

It's been three years, and Trisha and I are still together. In 2017, her apartment building in Temescal is sold to a developer who replaces the foundation. It's messy and noisy, endlessly disruptive. They're turning the building into condos. Steve and Lindsey move to Olympia. Trisha's parents offer to buy her a house. She has resisted this offer for many years but begins to consider it. There's stuff to work through—participating in the grotesque Bay Area housing market, becoming a property owner, being beholden to her parents in this way. I understand the concerns, but doling money to a landlord for the rest of your life isn't exactly a more ethically pure option.

But I'm scared too. Scared of the stability it offers me, a stability that's dependent on our relationship. Not a guarantee. I start unnecessary fights with Trisha, confusing this new security in housing with a loss of personal autonomy, which I make out to be her fault. I'm afraid I'll become comfortable and complacent, lose myself, afraid my politics will soften. To top it off, I've been at the same job for over a decade—a job I've wanted to leave for years but it pays well and offers tons of flexibility. Stuck in those golden handcuffs so I could afford my apartment in downtown Oakland.

We buy a hundred-and nine-year-old blue house in South Berkeley. It needs work. The previous owners, a family, lived there for thirty years. We make it our home. Trisha encourages me to finally leave my job, take a year off to work on my book and figure out what's next. She'll support me. You deserve it, she says. You've been through so much. I sit on the decision for a while, then I give my boss six months' notice.

Three days after my last day at work, I take a trip to Yucca Valley. I stay in a trailer in the desert that sits atop a ridge, overlooking a valley. I walk along the land that slopes below it. I sit outside the trailer and watch the sun set behind the ridge in the distance. I write and read and shoot video. I drive into a remote part of the Joshua Tree National Park and walk around. I experience a spiritual moment of communing with the land. It is December, 2018. I've been on hormones almost two years, and I'm eight months post top surgery. I am somewhat passing. I have broken through some blockages that seemed impossible just a few years before. I feel so grateful that I cry.

Back home, Charity visits from New York. Her sister lives in Santa Rosa. I pick her up, hang for a bit with her brother-in-law and two nephews, then drive her down to stay with me and Trisha for a night or two.

We take the 116 west, through Guerneville and Monte Rio, swoop down Highway 1 and over to Goat Rock Beach, down a weaving road that descends to the parking lot. Goat rock sits at the foot of the parking lot. There's a hill of rocks we climb on, rusted metal scattered among them, integrating with the natural landscape. To the right is an enclave where the ocean's pull is especially strong. A sign warns: "DANGER: This is one of the most deadly beaches in California." On either side are expansive areas for walking along the shore or sitting on the sand. Charity sits next to me clasping the tops of her knees. She leans back and reaches her arms out in front of her toward the ocean. She says, "what if the ocean impregnated me right now." Classic Charity. I take a pic and post it to Instagram later to ensure I remember the moment. I am a little bit in love with her. The friendship is something. We take breaks, need space, get irritated by one another, but other times the connection is taut, tingly, electric.

Back in Berkeley, we meet Morty at the Alchemy coffee shop on Alcatraz and Adeline. We each complain to him about how slow we are at writing our books. Morty says, stop making excuses! Just write. He's right, but it takes a while for me to admit it.

In 2017 and 2018, I write shards of poems beside my transition. I don't care to write *about* the transition (though of course, that comes through). I want the book to *be* it, to embody it. I want the book to bear the marks of my experience—messy, uncategorizable, noncontiguous, resistant to expected or dominant forms, ambivalent yet resolute in its right to exist. The book and the body in communion, two interwoven texts. They hold themselves open, where some of the beams and scars and scaffolding still show, inviting readers to peer further in. They will be gently resistant to misinterpretation, though misreadings will be made. Misreadings of the transitioned body, and of the open text, are inevitable. Nevertheless, the textual body and the warm supple book continue to demonstrate that they live—thrive, even—on their own self-made terms.

I resist the temptation to tell a clean tale of gender transition anyway, or to gratuitously narrate the content of my inner struggles. It scratches against me with every attempt, leaving splotchy patches, bloodied and raw. I compose pages upon pages and delete them all. What am I compelled to share for the sake of the book? And what is extraneous to the book, what alternate motivations come from my ego and its desire for... what? Legitimacy? Sympathy? Attention?

I still work on the collection of shards about gender and transition. I decide it belongs in the center of the book and title it "—", like a bridge. It lives there through many iterations. Then the house is renovated and the shards move to the front. I adjust to seeing it more like an opening, an on-ramp, an entryway. I change its name to "One." I'm reminded that I thought, from the very beginning, that the whole book is a bridge.

While I'm writing these fragments in 2017, I find a couple of old poems with named characters in them. I pull the characters to use in something new. They are various parts of me. I use them to tell a story.

I ask the figures to blow up a building—an old poem from ten years earlier that's been buried in a box. I feel bad for the characters that are stuck there. I want to help them get out. I set up the scene, provide the framework and conditions—like a good director, orchestrator, leader—and hang back to let them determine what happens. It takes a couple of years. Maybe more. Eventually, the question of what to do about the building, the old poem, the trapped characters in a box, gets answered another way.

But the characters stick. They show up in everything else I write. They become the rest of the book.

In early 2019, I adjust to not having a job. Unstructured time stretches out before me. I say I'm working on the book but I'm not doing much writing. I masturbate too much and clean the house all day. I feel lazy and uninspired. Trisha comes home from a toxic work environment, resentful of my freedom. To me the freedom feels like pressure. I'm turning forty this fall and I feel worthless. I'm always sullen, or angry, or defensive. Profound stress. I stop sleeping, but I don't heed the warning.

Samantha suggests we take a weekend in Point Arena at a retreat house that's currently empty. Yes, we go. The retreat house is called This Will Take Time. I arrive and set up my stuff in the upstairs office with a desk that overlooks a cascading green landscape. I go for a walk and follow faint desire lines through tall dry fields until I reach a pond. I read Glissant's *Poetics of Relation* and take pictures of the pages: IMAGINARY, APPROACHES, The Open Boat. On the page APPROACHES: "One way ashore, a thousand channels." Messages everywhere. I send cryptic texts to friends. I post on Instagram for lesbian visibility day, saying that, while I don't feel I can claim that identity category anymore, the fifteen years I lived as a dyke are still very much a part of me. I realize in this moment I have figured something out that I've been struggling with for years. It's personal but feels revolutionary. I figured out how to let myself be.

Samantha arrives and the weekend is great. She cooks and I do dishes. We do our own thing during the day and spend evenings together, drinking wine and talking shit. I feel activated and energized. I'm writing the book, I think. In my sleepless nights I feel like I'm writing the book even though I'm not doing any writing.

My mind spins on the book and everything inside and around me. Everything feels connected. The book is my life and I'm writing it by living it. But the book starts writing me. Something else slips in too.

On the way home from the retreat house, I lose myself. Disappear into the folds of the brain, some kind of neurochemical swirl. A manic episode with psychotic symptoms lasting about a month. Two trips to the psychiatric facility and one trip to jail. I spend the second half of 2019 and all of 2020 piecing myself back together.

The narrative segments of the book span years where collective anxiety boils. White supremacists brazenly taking the streets. The Trump years—every few months a new assault. At the same time, more resistance movements, more mutual aid, more learning and sharing skills. To some, Twitter has become the central battle-ground between reactionaries and revolutionaries. Out in the world, the clamp of power tightens its grip.

In a faraway place—everywhere and nowhere—the residents of a virtual town participate in a constant gathering.

Their bodies are sedentary while their minds deliriously rush and skip around. Like tiny iron shards to a magnet, they cling all at once to positive and negative pulls. They bathe in their own glistening excrement as they produce more and more—like a pack of pigs in a mud-filled pit, they roll around oinking and squealing, spewing bile on each other and lapping it up.

We sit side by side on a felled tree outside the village
The marsh is a slimy green and the air is still
You slap your leg as a mosquito weaves through the hair to bite skin
The only way in is through the earholes the mouth the anus
You say. I shake my head. there must be something else

I pick up a twig, crack it, and peel the outer layer. I crack it again and again until there are tiny pieces. I collect the pieces in a small cluster in front of me.

The marsh is thick, a heavy stench bubbles up from its depths,
a vat of soup
You slap your arm and wave your hand back and forth next
to your ear
We watch a worm slither out from the marsh onto land

Reminding us we were there once, slithering on our bellies before
we had limbs
Before air was a thing we paid for

"The end of the world" you say
Is the rise of a new order
We don't yet know what it will be
"It will not be what we imagine"

I'm looking at the thick sludge gurgling
Wishing to be back inside it, where I don't have to regard things
so closely
Just climb on top of whatever's having a moment and kick it
down—
A lifeline for my basest self

On your knees a large picture book lies open, depicting the swamp
we were born into, and out and from, a million stories ago.

When you found the book lying in the sand and lifted it

I turn the page to see an illustration of its insides—organs and
tissue, beams and concrete, veins and bones, originary forms—the
neck still tense.

I crawl out of the swamp and die instantly on land. I die over and
over for several billion years until, one day, I crawl out and live.

Marionettes leap through the crowd, their pointy hats and shoes flop around with the rest of their rubbery limbs, poking a finger into the ribcage, up a nostril, in the warm crevice between buttocks. They cackle, hop about, climb walls, and swing from poles as the flames surrounding the town grow larger, suffocating the space where we once slept, where we fucked with abandon, where we once threw our bodies on a line.

You take everything so seriously, you whisper.
I know, I say a little too loud.

But mostly we're sitting in silence
Beside the swamp
It's not yet dark enough to lift our heads back and consult with the stars. Their movements are reflected inside our nervous systems, and in the web of relations that tie everyone to another. These fine threads—whether taut or loose, swaying or vibrating—tell us enough of what we need to understand.

Occasionally we hear a rustle of leaves or a branch crack or the scurrying of animal legs, see the fainting light through trees.

The square has changed. The stage, no longer—
The concert hall will be moving locations.

A young boy walks through a field pulling livestock attached to a long-threaded rope.

Jackals prey further out at a distance, waiting for rejected carnage that's been exiled to outer spheres and towns, hovering for an evening repast.

A worm slithers out of the sludge onto land. It reaches my pile of sticks and starts climbing the hill, stops to check out the view from the peak.

Structures continue to crumble. The frame of a house tilts. Flames leap around the yard.

A car zooms by
It spins me around and I fall

Yes, I've been proclaiming loudly my pronouncements from the middle of the road, in the middle of a city, to all who'll hear—to whoever will throw me a bone.
Yes, it was my attempt to grab some attention in the center of a city where everyone is doing the same in the center of their own.

People keep walking to their destinations on the sidewalks, scooters fly past, bicyclists yell over their shoulders, cars speed around.

I used to walk my little body through these crowded streets with a fist raised to the sky. Now I watch everyone around me yell at everyone around them, still with a fist to the sky.

Now I'm followed in my car by a few pickup trucks. I think they're tracking me. I pull over to the side of the road and walk down a path toward the ocean. I sit by a small pond and lie back. Look up at the sun and the sky. Euphoria blankets me. I'm linked up with the universe. I understand everything about time and life and the cosmos. On the internet, everyone is speaking directly to me. They have identified me and are all honing in. I get lost in the car because I try to find my way home without the maps because I don't want my phone to track me anymore. The music changes and I don't recognize the song that's playing. Someone took over my phone and they're feeding music into the car as a message. I turn around a couple of times thinking they're trying to re-route me. I speak aloud in the car: *please leave me alone.* I think, what if I drive really fast into a tree to make it stop.

Back home, Trisha and friends are against me. They give me pills to make me sleep. In the morning I hear them whispering outside my room. I grab my hoodie, shove some cash in my pocket, and rush out the door. Trisha chases me down the block but she can't catch up. I walk around in my neighborhood for hours thinking I'm not alive anymore. Everyone else is dead, too. But we have to play a game in order to get back to our real lives. Some don't know the game they're playing. I spend time at the neighborhood home-less camp talking with people. They think my name is Seth so they call me Seth. I look for a way out of town, maybe to the desert. I won't come back. I go home with messages for allies—Grace and Buuck—as if there's a secret war taking place. There is. But one is never certain who is a real ally. I punch a cop in the face. He entered my house. I think there are only two but after I punch him I'm surrounded by, how many, five? Six? On the floor in my home face down screaming, with cuffs on my wrists and a knee in my back.

I'm white, so I live. They strap me into an ambulance and drive me to the county-run psychiatric facility where I sit in a room with forty other people wandering around barely attended to for eight hours. When I'm released from the mental hospital I'm brought straight to jail. The cop pressed charges. I sit in a solitary cell for ten hours. Then I'm released and Trisha is waiting outside with friends and my sister who has flown in from across the country. Friends rally to help in my recovery. I refuse to get help. I say, I'm fine, it was just an isolated thing. A month later, Julian is coming for a visit and something snaps. It happens again. I'm lying in the backyard, my body filled with pills. I almost die.

I want my life to count. I'm the only one who's really watching. So I do it for me.

Reader, have I told you the car that swiped me was driven by a friend? She wanted to make sure I was safe. She was caring for me in this way. I know it.

Another friend, Samantha, lifts me in my deluded state from the burning ashes of my faltering mind. She transports me safely home so that I think she or I are gods or messengers of someone powerful, someone who has set out to destroy me or make me king.

The scrapes on my arms heal quickly after the fall. I get up as the busy street carries on. My body dissolves into a digital avatar. My pointed ears stick up like a fox. My tail curls in a spiral. My big eyes bulge. I lift myself up the way an animated character would, furry hands flat on the ground, back curled, neck rolled up as arms push off the ground and I stand. I sway. The head bobs. I shake it fiercely and get in a stance.

I look down at my outstretched arms and see a shiny luster on the scrapes and scars, on the broken capillaries, my pale olive skin now with a silver sheen, like liquid metal pouring through veins. I turn metallic.

If we're going this way, we may go further, all the way? There's more to go. We could try to be prepared. Persuaded? We could try that. I'm not having it. No I won't go.
Instead, I die by the side of the road.

In a quiet room filled with shrieking voices
I think *I need to choose*
to be with myself
So I walk over to the windows and close
them and draw the curtains. I put the phone down.
I go to the networks and minimize the windows, one by one, tabs
floating downward to the dock
I gently press the laptop
closed—

But I wasn't in the psychiatric facility this time. If I were, there'd be no windows—just a hallway I slept in with twelve others facing a huge desk where two nurses sat and ignored us. We're told this is where the well-behaved people stay and if we cause any trouble we'll be sent into the big room where forty people are wandering around unattended. I sleep in a blue plastic fold-out chair for three nights side-by-side with the others. I think I'll get out after

the seventy-two-hour hold but they admit me into the hospital
for a few more days. It's a place with no resources, no programs,
nothing to do. Outdoor time is occasional and the outdoor area
is a caged cement block. The weekend nurse locks the individual
bathroom and tells me I can't use the men's room. Appealing on
the basest level, I gesture to my facial hair and say, look at me, you
want me to use the women's room? She says yes, it's for your own
safety.

I continue to use the men's. And the old white woman with a hole
in her face who'd yell "get that he-she away from me" and the
nurses say, *now now, stop that*, and then continue to call ERIKA in
front of everybody at mealtimes, causing me to cringe and then
walk up to receive my plastic tray of food. And in the other room,
with forty people roaming around, a young man muttering to himself with a blanket draped on his shoulders followed around by a
nurse. That was the first time, before I went to jail, before I took
the pills, before I crumbled.

This is what it was, I think.
No, this is what it is. Everyday.
Every day that I'm here, it's still like that in there.

The swamp draws near again. It's got a tide
I look over at you for something, a look or a sign, of what, of what
to do?

Then I see that the woods we are in, apart from the carnival
is not separate from it at all but rather inside it, a part of it—

I realize that we're aflame too, along with everyone else.
It seems to me that whoever was sitting next to me knew this already.

A pack of marionettes rushes over to us and starts stomping around in a circle. One of them runs up and shoves you into the swamp. You sink into its depths. I'm left alone, with my head in my hands. Sometime later I open my eyes and see you emerging from the thick sludge—there you are—a marionette yourself.

You crouch in front of me, put your face up to mine, and spit.
I don't wipe it off. Your spit hangs from my face. I deserve it.

Thinking I was on the outside of something while being right there in it.
There's more work to do. To make it be so.

So I climb into the swamp. Or I slither out from it. Doesn't matter.
The carnival is the easiest place to go. The swamp recedes more and more.
The marionettes are gone.
We are not to be trifled with.
The book lies in the sludge, open and waiting.

together

In the imaginary, I paint the language of the Northern California coast against my body.

Hue walks into the poem posing as me. Seldom visits her there. He pokes around the rooms and takes a turn sitting on the toilet seat, hunched over, with his face in his hands. It feels familiar but it's different. We were there before me and the crew—working on a different experiment.

I start another story. This time, the characters are not destroying an old poem. They are assisting me in the composition of new narratives. I pull them together again. I meet them at the coast.

Why must I send others into the den of imagination to create, or to destroy what I create? *Destroy/Rejoice,* Libel says, in the original poem.

Seeing into some future I can't perceive, where I take a half-step turn and feel the pressure that weighs on me in the End Times Review Journal of my final collection.

The characters re-emerge. They walk through the curtain.

There's a cave at the top of a cliff above the edge of the ocean. Meet me there.

I've never been before but I'm on my way now. To meet you.

Seldom is driving to get there. The maps app on his phone helps him avoid whatever construction or traffic lies ahead. It guides him on an alternate route and he dutifully follows. Passes a Coast Guard training facility. The gate and insignia. He drives through a neighborhood with identical houses, pale in color, plain in style, lined in perfect rows. The streets are empty of people.

A blue pickup truck tails him through the neighborhood. At the end of the road he turns right and the truck turns left. Now he's on a winding road lined by tall trees. The ocean is to his left—he can't see it, but he knows it's there. Another truck, white, with two white men inside. Eyes on the rearview mirror more than on the road in front of him. It feels like he's being followed. Half a mile later, another blue truck behind the white one. The white truck turns off. It's all coordinated. I've been marked. Bands of armed militias proliferating across the country. The music app on his phone shifts to Alice Coltrane's *Journey to Satchidananda* as his paranoia begins to heighten. Good stuff swirls through his ears, opening portals in the space of the car, but the bad stuff swims in too. He sees a turnout and swerves into it. Trucks boom past.

I'm just a regular person stopping for a pee break—take a little walk, stretch out the legs, he thinks—to those who are tracking me. No one's around but I can feel them watching. I hold something, the understanding of a mystery, and this makes me dangerous, because I am something they want to destroy, annihilate—indeed become, though they can't—and this is my fault too. I take a sip of water, get out of the car, visit the outhouse, and start down the path toward the ocean.

After his twenty-minute walk, Seldom gets back in the car. A dark green Jeep turns onto the road in front of him. It's here to lead him to safety. He gets out of the car and walks to meet the others outside the cave. At the lower ridge, an abandoned house. A screen door hangs by a hinge. Stacks of chopped wood. He wants to peer through a dirty window but he's already running late. He keeps up the path toward the peak. Piles of tires, car parts, rusted junk dapple the landscape.

Hue is already at the top of the cliff, waiting outside the cave for the others to arrive. Of course they're the first to get there. Of course everyone else will be late. A memory resurfaces and Hue floats with it for a while, until a gust of wind hits their face.

In the cloud of memory, Hue is walking home from work at the coffee shop in Rockridge—Cole Coffee, formerly Royal—to their apartment on the corner of Telegraph and Alcatraz. A small studio apartment in the same building as the Ethiopian restaurant Café Colucci, one block from the White Horse bar. It's the first place they move into when arriving in Oakland in 2005. Something like

$575 a month for rent. The apartment has a kitchen, a long narrow hallway, a bathroom, and a room for their bed and desk. Off the room, a small porch. The cat climbs up the wooden slats of the lattice fence surrounding the porch and sits on top, never going down the other side to explore. This memory pushes against another from the same time and place.

Walking home from work, I see a note lying on the sidewalk. It reminds me of a note someone once wrote to me. A gust of wind rattles against the window by my desk.

Hue leans over the side rail, looking down at their clasped hands. They take a long deep breath and let it out, returning from the memory to the present. Something in their body is buzzing like an electricity that keeps them connected to the beyond.

Venn rounds the corner, pulling a toothpick from her mouth and flicking it away. She wears a leather jacket, short floppy hair, and a warm sadness in her eyes. She walks up to Hue with an awkward swagger, smiles, says hi. Hue nods their head. Venn runs a hand through her hair, then bites a nail. Three seagulls dip toward the water.

When Seldom finally arrives, Hue and Venn are huddled together against the wind. He apologizes for being late. He tells them about the drive he just had, following the alternate course that his phone led him on, getting tailed by creepy trucks. They remind him he's not in Oakland anymore. They laugh.

He leaves out the part about pulling over to the side of the road and walking toward the ocean. Doesn't mention the tree he spent time with, gnarled branches extending out like a canopy cradling him at a remove from the path, and the half dozen houses facing the ocean in an arc. How he continues to feel watched with those houses behind me. How he could get shot in the back of the head while walking toward the ocean and no one would know. He turns around instead of going all the way to the end and retraces his steps, with the arc of houses facing him and the gnarled tree coming up on my left. He sees a couple on their porch reading the paper, pretending to not see him. I'm not in Oakland. I'm somewhere else, another place. I'm not even here.

LET'S GO, Venn calls over to Chase, who's crouching behind a
metal pipe poking at something with a stick. Chase stands up and
rushes over to where the rest are waiting. Seldom tilts his head
back. It's almost time, he says.

Samuel appears out of nowhere, with lighter fluid and a grin.
Okay, let's do it.

I collect words from everyone and cradle them in my hands, roll
them up into a ball and pop them in my mouth, chewing the sky
into place above us.

Venn opens the book in her lap.
Hue tilts their laptop screen so the glare doesn't interfere.

We thought we were the first and would be the last,
Chase says.

We ushered in our legacy because we had the legitimacy and
resources to do it. To make it be so. And it was so, but only in our
imaginary.

BLIZZARD. Someone speaks the word and it becomes
an element to contend with in the sound between our ears
on the other side, a tension.

Hue types fast. Venn flips to another page.

The movement is a bus. Intention determines its character. Action steers its direction. Passengers come along for the ride. Some stay on and others hop off. Some might hop off and on, depending on where they're at in life. When they're on, they judge those who are off. When they're off, they judge those who are on. A few people take turns navigating. Drivers don't always listen to suggested instructions. The changing of drivers isn't always pretty. Some people push against the direction the bus is heading, no matter what. One paints the outside of the bus while another fills it with gas. Someone else cleans the windshield while another looks under the hood. Two people sit next to each other in the back row, sharing music. One person sits alone writing in a notebook. Another stares out the window. Four people engage in a heated debate. One imagines the bus tilting its nose into the sky.

They stop typing. They look up from the page.

It begins with destruction and ends with beginning,
Seldom says,

A story told without having to tell it—already here.

It's time, they say.

I climb on top of a tree stump. Figures emerge from the brush to gather around and watch. I stand tall and straight, as a vertical line from ground to sky. I speak—but what can I say?

Seldom walks over dragging an axe along the dirt. The cave howls at my back.

They're watching. They want to relish the moment. When it's over they'll enter the cave and write the script. Fuck each other all night in there as I open my legs for a new kind of emergence—going inside instead of coming out.

Seldom takes a decisive swing. He strikes at the top of my head, a single downward motion. A crackling sound like shredded pieces of wood. I splinter—

One and Null, two sides born into the dirt.

Null falls to their knees coughing. One rolls on the ground and curls.
Each attached to the other with cords pulled by someone else.
When One grabs at a tube, Null whips it at the onlookers.
When Null sings in a hum, One's vocal chords vibrate.

There's Chase, standing at the base of the ridge.

Tall trees line the crest in the distance. He can't see beyond the boundary of the trees but he knows he will have to get past them. He recalls a time where someone walked beside him along a fence discussing her dissertation. He was a child then, so how could this be? Was it a dream? It's in his mind as a memory.

Chase wonders if she was ever there in the first place, but whoever was discussing her dissertation was a remnant. He remembers the setting, the scene. "It happened," Chase says, "but the image of her is a faded line-drawing blurred in my mind."

Hue nods, as if they're listening. They're walking a few paces ahead. Chase pauses to scan the trees atop the ridge.

Hue recalls a piece of writing from their past.

They arrive home from work, drop their keys on the mantle, drop their bag on the floor, walk up the stairs. They hear splashing from the bathroom and look in: Libel in the tub. Hue enters, turns the toilet seat cover down and sits on top of it. They put their head in their hands.

If I could make things happen other than writing about, or make the writing make things happen, Hue says, the old wooden apartment I rented with a friend in Portland, running into the old landlady, having something else to do, getting back late and having to leave early—

Hue paces up and down the hallway. Libel sips from a glass of red wine and spills some into the bubble bath.

And then one day the neighbor rang our doorbell with a note in their hand, a note someone had written to me. The neighbor found it in their yard. It caused them to worry, to come over and ask if I was okay. Standing outside the door, holding out the note. And, of course, I recognize it.

The light has shifted
it is a warm day in February
T watches television from her
laptop, with ear buds in, the screen
glows back at her
my gaze lands on her face
she is smiling, a pleasant countenance

My countenance doesn't smile much,
not for lack of pleasure and privilege
in this life but rather
a seriousness behind the curtains
that finds gutters and alleyways of composition
to seep through
like the blood of a slaughtered pig
under the moonlight
forms streams that trickle
between the townspeople's feet

Someone listens
to music between their ears,
enters the head and bounces
the sounds around inside

Bridge between ears, pulled from volume, an amplitude

In the ocean, the group plays badminton with dead slugs.

They throw some toward us so we can whack at them with our rackets. Venn roams in shallow waters, bent at the waist, swiping her hands along the mud packed floor. Hue puts a slug in their mouth and lets it dangle out between their lips, smiling around it, then spitting it out. Chase splashes over to catch one but misses, falls into an oncoming wave, arms flailing as he tumbles into the water and pops back out. Hue finds another slug and tosses it over. Chase throws three at once.

Seldom gets a few good whacks.
At most of the ones that come toward me, I swing and miss.

The surf is getting stronger.

Someone loses a son to the ferocious waves. Or was it a daughter. I try to swim out to the child but I fail.

Even the mother won't let me go any further. She says, you would be gone too, and what good would that've done.

I wonder what she means about driving on the edge where land and water meet.

Venn implies there's something else. Perhaps of the road drawing out and forth, along a bridge, with velocity or amplitude.

I take you up there knowing you'll appreciate the view.
And you do.

After we round the corner, we slow down. Hundreds of people are milling around, while many cops act like their presence creates order. A tree is cut down. People stand on either side of the tree, holding a saw, and pull back and forth until the tree falls. It isn't a very tall tree, it's short and stout, and takes a long time to fell.

T sighs, what am I going to put here?
she is writing a book
we are sitting in the living room
her in a chair, me on the couch
I'm not writing much
I am looking around the room
as if something will come to me
a shifted position
from the edge of a raft
charting through new waters
this house we moved into, making it
home, a craft floating atop the muddy swamp
of this city's nightmare

Wanting the ocean of the city
to sink and all of our rafts to rise. to wake the story
out of its dream and re-write itself

Null seals the doors of history closed.
Declares *step off the land!* in a booming voice that radiates.

All the players on the field stop in mid-run. All realize the ball
they've been kicking around was never there. Their eyes move in
erratic circles. "Now what of this dream, nightmare, that isn't a
dream." Voices float like invisible clouds around their heads.

Null stops counting, which means time stops. Time is returned to
the bodies.

But the thing that remains is the memory of a slight sensation
that has to do with proximity—one who breathes fire into
a pointed horror, as if one is to confess where one came from
and the conditions that brought them to where they stand

A conversation takes place between doubles.

Null and One have a few of those: language the other can't receive, something watched but not seen, listened to but not heard. A few intentionally placed words, a hidden network of code slapping its vocabulary around.

A way across the line
comes in the form of a dream or expressed as one

Legs strong. Loose knees. Back firm. Arms arced slightly at the sides. Tongue resting lightly behind the upper front teeth. Top of the head, soft and receptive. I bow—to the sky, to the earth, and to the teacher.

The idea of the line
is more linear than a line itself
which is nothing,
a fantasy

Move arms in large circles, forward ten times, backward ten times. Slap arms around midsection. Rub temples. Rub sides of waist and pelvis. Rub each side of the neck. Stand on one foot.

It's not simple, to encounter
the world and leave
things out. The omitted parts
accumulate, build an edifice
of all the stories that could have been told
making a history of their own—
the unspoken tower

Suddenly, the building bursts into flames.

A fire rises around us and we are made whole in the image of a language emptied out like tufts of billowing smoke through windows.

Driving miles on
the coastline along a ridge. She never
finishes the sentence
that dangles—

From the cliff, a string of words
hang where you can find them

If the story needs another
ending, climb the rock
to a new string
and grab it.

I pour my thin noxious blood down his throat. Thirsty Samuel gets up.

In the verifiable pursuit of no one, he turns his eyes down and refuels. Hue stands next to Seldom close, smacks his knee and enters the room.

I haven't arrived yet. I'm there as a vision.

Seldom looks into the blast, the gaping emptiness of the old apartment building from the previously written score, years old and discarded.

These are my friends, he says, though they do not contain my friends—they're imaginary.

We've been stuck in these worn-down streets and blasted buildings. We never see through our own windows or are seen by the readers peering in. These words that never made it, the fellows come from there.

The blast puts fire in the gut, throat, neck, chest. A wanting from Hue's eyes signals it's time to leave. Destroy the old bedrooms, dolls, and furniture sets, cars and model planes, destroy for thirst, old dolly. Seldom grabs the last piece of fruit, a nectarine.

Still thirsty, Samuel guzzles the blood that pours from my shoulder as we run from the rubble.

"It isn't fair."
No it's not.

In my dream, I tell the story and Seldom listens
But in the story he's the one who dictates terms

They walk through the public concourse, step out onto the street, cram into the car, then arrive at their destination, enter the old apartment building, up the spiral staircase, every so often a creak beneath the foot, and at the top, hand against door, a push, body moves through—

The figures are sitting in the living room of the old apartment. I've already left, crawling through the cave to emerge elsewhere, and let them have their space. I am never too far away, though. I can hear their voices through the dull roar of the sea, through the wind and the thin bird calls, through the sand between my fingers.

Chase pulls open the curtains and cracks the window. Let's get a little air in here.

I describe the scene we are settling into. The description appears in my previous book, now becoming the draft of a future book— one that may come to be, or that will never be:

"I see people sitting around cross-legged on the floor in a room. They are talking and arguing about concepts and strategies I can only partially grasp. They want to play the arsonists in a future experiment. I do too. We don't want to predetermine too much although some basic premises must be agreed upon in advance.

They all talk at the same time. Their voices are insistent and contradictory and impatient. They are unmaking a reality into a possibility, then a probability, then an incontrovertible fact, as their desires become words."

It starts with a poem, Seldom says. Everyone listens as the narration unfolds. *It begins with destruction and ends with beginning—*

Almost immediately, an interruption.

HUE:
I wake at 4am thinking about my job
can't go back to sleep
work taking time from life / takes time from sleep
takes sleep from life
No matter how often I see my friends I wonder where are my friends? Which of them, who, and why? When I die I'll be released from my body—the brain, a part of the body that fails sometimes, works hard on insignificant things, short-circuited, circular edging, distracted maneuvers. The way some people need a kind of amplified conflict in order to feel okay, feel close to others, in order to go on. My need to not have conflict amplified, that messy kind you can't extricate from. I'm there on the other side each time back again I try from another angle. In the glass, I look. It hurts to know.

Sometimes I think I want more than what most people think is possible.

The dawn pulls itself up
through windows
Hue, we'll be here all night—
It could carry on well into the next day
With the dawn ever upon us

Are you listening, Venn lies on the ground with an arm swaying in
the air, lets it flop down and asks, to everyone, in the frame

CHASE:
If you hold your thumb down for long enough
—see someone squirming under it
You'd have to bother to look
See how you hover over another?
Nobody wants to see *that*!

They writhe under the thumbs of others—
that is what they see

The writhing I've done, sure I've screamed about it all,
slurred and spat my hardships, a fair share
Now I breathe it out processed
Still hurts, but it's mine

The square has changed. The stage, no longer.
I spit into the mouths of others without their knowing it.
They slurp their tongues into mine when I'm most unaware.

Everything left to destroy—and destroying itself—the ALL of it
Every way you are right now. Every way you hide. Are you ready?

The thing about glass is that it's so breakable. A foul, shit-clogged mind is the tricky thing,

Chase says,

Trust is gone
but I saved a little for you
Wonder if you'll have any to spare yourself
for another—

the thorn at the side bites
point to the originator of the thorn, ok
can't stop talking about it, dead writing—
but friend, what would you do without that thorn?
you'd be like them

HUE:
I know, I'm supposed to not care. Or perform a knowing. At least I could pretend. Everyone's made of the same stuff, differently arranged. You're drawn to one and repelled by another. It all depends on where you're at in the moment, that's it, do you match *compositionally*? In most cases it's not what is being said—

You hate seeing reflections of yourself out there. You're obsessed with the aspects of yourself that you hate. So you hate the person who externalizes it. But you're drawn to them. You think about them a lot. It's sensual. You want the stuff they have (you have it too). You hate the stuff they do—it's also yours. It shows up differently. It shows you up.

Same shit, always has been,
says Hue.
In times of crisis, under duress, people splinter into groups—
some cling to power, some fight against it, and the many
who coast safely at a remove from the fight—
or suffer and die below it.

"Which side are you on?" drifts in from crowds outside the window.

Broad strokes, these sides, Venn says. In each are many splinters
and fragments. The fight is everywhere, with some pleasure and
rest between. You go hard on some issues and turn your back on
others, shut out some people and make allowances for others.
And what if some of the coasters are fighting in a form you can't
see?

Is that what the liberal says? 'Cause I ain't a liberal,
says Hue to Chase
says Chase to himself
says I, says you,
into the flat
bright
abyss

You hold the perfect line on everything, in precisely the correct
way, to the exact right degree. Of course you do.

Venn looks up—
Who?

What was that?

Venn pulls a piece of hair from her face, curls it behind an ear. Everyone is breathing. A cool breeze rushes in, the curtain sways.

As for me, it's hard to say anything definitive knowing that someday I'll disagree with it—which I will, because my thinking evolves. The possibility that others will toss it away later, or worse, put it on display as a kind of theoretical failure. All the times I didn't share my thinking in the moment for fear of being wrong, a lack of participation in a process of thought—the personal, of course, but also collective—which is how I most learn and grow. *I get there anyway*, I tell myself, *by watching and learning from others.* I tell myself a lot of things to justify an easier course.

When I do speak out, I sputter a little too forcefully like I know what I'm saying, even if I'm just testing out how it sounds. Later while alone, I think through it twice, and perhaps reach a new conclusion. But when others make a claim I disagree with, there they stay, frozen in that pose. I don't give them the benefit of a similar kind of growth.

I dip a brush into the rushing streams of my nervous system, splash my insecurities onto the canvas of their blank empty face. I remake them in my self-image—they are ugly, wrong, BAD.

That's you—
Me?

That's me, says Hue.

I think about this a lot, says Chase.

They speak over there with an added verve—half-baked, reactive, disembodied, unforgiving—it's not all bad, but it makes me want to not talk at all.

So here we are talking. Me and you.

This is how it is, I say. Either the sun is shining or it's not. Whatever you prefer. I'll have to decide the weather. You'll have to go along with it. The sun pokes out after we turn the corner, just after we decide it might rain. Take what you need and leave the rest, let it slide away along the rocks, algae, stream, thumb, holding patterns of hell, forest, cloud, jazz record, newspaper, systems of oppression, metal show, listserv, hologram, horror movie, rotary phone, public restroom, the noise of it.

We're walking together at a reasonable pace.
Stay with me here.

It was only seconds that you slipped
I stumbled and fell on my hands then pulled up

Quick

Don't forget a day is long
Attention's sho—
Life
is very long

even the short ones

We mourn the lives that are short, but they win—the young
ones—
gone before they're corrupted any more

The rush of life shortens time
you know this
but time moves at the same pace, while the body
forgets to live it

MY BRIDGE IS DEAD?
Over what ridge

Where we stood, at the beginning and end of the world.

My bridge was dead as soon as the ink dried. *But it's a living entity
inside the framework.*

Someday the world that's alive in my mind will end. Nobody else
has it but me, Hue says, thinking they were the first to say that

Where did you go?

I'm right here, Chase says, while spewing fragments of himself
over the walls as I'm trying to eat my dinner.

I could hear better if you allowed me more space.

Who the fuck're you?

In the meantime, you think this is a joke while I'm tossing myself into sewage pipes, driving my car into a tree, running through unfamiliar fields, planning my escape—

You don't give me much credit, do you?
Unless I keep up a compelling performance of my own.
There are other things to do.
Sometimes I tap my toes to the beat
Sing a song or spin around for you to see

It's not everything. The LAND and the NIGHT SKY remind me. I am thus reminded.

To end with obscurity and death, after all. Why *wouldn't* everyone want that?

What a life you could live—if you knew from the start—
that you would be forgotten.

You didn't give me a chance to say my piece, though.

Didn't I?

What else do you say to yourself when alone with the rest of the world?

A gust of wind blows through the window. Venn walks over and pulls it closed.

Ten years or a century go by.

They're still in the room, gnawing on crumbs of dialogue held in their mouths a little too long or not long enough. We may return to the scene again.

Seldom finally concedes to my earlier request.

The house is rotting from the inside out. They enter it, the poem—the demolition crew does. They walk from the apartment building to the derelict site where they destroy what was built.

A trashed warehouse. A large, empty space. A chair in the center.

The end of an era.
He said that too, while sitting in the tub,
Hue reminds us—
It's the only way to know.
Doesn't mean you can't write it differently.

Hue leans against the crumbling cement wall as the rest get to work. She positions herself just out of sight from Libel, who has now been led to the chair and firmly placed in it. She joined the group, and it saved her. But someone will need to be sacrificed.

Your process is an odd one, Seldom says.
I didn't have the duct tape unrolled in time,
Says Venn, as she ducks under the half-open garage door to enter.
He did it to himself.

I couldn't watch, but I had to be there.

He strapped Libel's ankles to the chair.
"You thought you were getting out of this."
The margin of error tightens.
Creaking steps in a home that isn't yours.
A naked man sitting in your tub,
A reflection of you that you'll never be—

Tear a piece of tape with teeth, the shrill rip
Behind the wall, another wall painted yellow.
Then the wrists, one by one, to the metal chair, taping him down
As he was steadily breathing. He seemed to enjoy it.
Seldom steps back to look. Libel, tell me a story. One last time.

*One came home. Dropped their keys on the mantle. Dropped their bag
on the floor. Opened a bag of popcorn. Opened a beer. Someone heard
the commotion and came downstairs. One looked up to find someone
standing there naked, dripping on the cold linoleum floor. Someone
winked. One rolled their eyes. This was who you wanted to be. Someone
you wanted, one you wanted to be. In your frustration you went blank,
obfuscating half stories with no reward, no meaning, no core. Ripples
in skin, shortened breath. I kept things amusing for a time but you
grew more and more angry. The anger came in fits of rage, you were*

jealous, you wanted to be famous like me, you wanted to be smart like me, beautiful and belligerent like me, you wanted to want everything. Yes, Libel, it's true, I did want that. I keep the stone in my pocket to ground me in my needs. *Do you hear me, Seldom, I'm stuck. Libel, sit still. I haven't finished taping your ankles to the chair.*

The tape comes round from back of head over lips
Almost covers the nostrils, enough to feel air expressed against itself
Kindling in the corner, the fellows that brought us here
Venn, an expert in explosives. Hue as the backup.
Chase might not make it. He knew it, too. He volunteered himself, a way out.
Samuel makes an uninvited appearance.

Detonation complete.
Did everyone get out before the blast?
Seldom, where is Libel? What have you done?

Desert Song

I drive to the desert and stay in a trailer at the edge of a ridge overlooking a valley. I wake early and open the trailer door to a view of the sunrise. I step outside to greet the land. The silence of the desert turns me inward. My story of the desert will stay there—carrion for the birds.

I close the laptop and meet Evan for a drink at a new gay bar in downtown Oakland. He's sitting at the end of the bar facing the front door. I approach him and say hi. As I remove my jacket, I see that his feet are resting comfortably on the lowest rungs of the stool next to him, so I place my jacket on the next stool over and sit. The bartender approaches and I order a beer.

The side of the mountain is like a waste yard. A mound of tires and car parts litter the view. A house sits in the distance. Large rocks sprinkled with white bird droppings are scattered along the land above the ocean. The guests follow a path over a lower ridge and up to the peak. From the top they can see a great distance, tall trees lining a crest beyond, the ocean below. One by one, they arrive, settling around the opening of the cave. You can hear the ocean from here. The air hums.

I tell Evan I haven't yet sent this piece to Eric for the latest issue of *Amerarcana* that he's guest editing for Nick. He shakes his head. He says he sent his in two weeks ago. I say, Trisha did too. I guess you are the good ones. Evan says you are one of the tardy ones.

You can almost hear him say that, can't you, in that cadence he speaks with: "tardy ones."

Seldom worries he'll be late, but he arrives just on time. He tips his hat so the brim shades sunlight from his eyes. His stance is casual. He looks like he strolled in from a classic noir film, one I've never seen. It is an image renewed for the current moment, but not in that tacky way that resembles a gaudy gentrification of classic looks. It's more messy and sloppy, not quite right, the way a person who is a replica from your subconscious looks as it wakes from a decades-long slumber to find itself alert and reminiscent of some older time, some other dimension, maybe a dream state. Not really there. A segment of yourself only you can see in a particular hue.

Hue stands at the edge of the cliff, leaning over the rail. It's Hue who first arrives in the house ten years ago to open the window and look outside, to first see the structure as a book or a story. Venn turns the corner, walks up and shakes her head. She casts a shadow on my face by stepping between the sun and me when she enters. Chase is crouching on the ground to get a close-up shot of something behind a pipe. Samuel looks up and down the valley, back and forth, as a stream of water courses between his feet.

When Evan first hears me read an early version of this work at Amy's house, he says with assurance that these figures are poets. I say, how interesting that you think so—they are not. Now, a year later in our conversation at the bar, he repeats himself: "oh, that piece of writing with the poets." He says this as I'm in the middle of saying something else, so I don't interrupt myself to correct him. After completing my thought, I want to go back and set the record straight but I worry that I'll sound defensive, which will do nothing to change his mind. I let it go.

Seldom stops to take a sip, then goes back to typing:

I collect words from everyone and cradle them in my hands, roll them up into a ball and pop them in my mouth, chewing the sky into place above us.

Blizzard. Someone speaks the word and it becomes
an element between our ears to contend with
on the other side of a wall, reverberating tension
in the air that hums

As I write the above—I mean, as I copy and paste it from a previous version—I think, maybe they are poets, after all? Who am I to say they're not? What bothers me is not that they might be poets but that Evan seems to think they're poets modeled on people we know. That's not true. Though there *are* two poets in this piece modeled on people we know—him and me.

Our bodies cradle the corner of the bar as we talk. We talk about our writing and the woes of being writers, we talk about friends we have in common, places we want to travel to, books we've been reading, thinkers we disagree over, his Grindr hookups in foreign countries, and the bad poetry readings we've had to sit through. I place one of my feet on the lower rungs of the stool between us, sometimes angle myself closer to him for a while and then straighten out to face the bar directly. When it gets crowded, I slide over onto the empty stool between us to make room for others. At first it feels too close, but after a moment of adjustment we're fine.

I think again about the piece of writing that's not ready to be sent to Eric. It begins like this:

I'm driving to the desert listening to Karlheinz Stockhausen's *Licht*, a twenty-nine-hour opera cycle for seven days of the week. I'm specifically listening to *Samstag aus Licht* ("Saturday from Light"). It lasts three hours and eighteen minutes. I'm not enjoying it very much but I listen all the way through. I'm driving along a frustrating two-lane stretch of I-5 and the cars in the left lane refuse to move over

It breaks right there and turns into a poem-rant that lasts a page and a half about how terrible drivers are, which obviously does not belong in the piece of writing but just had to pour out, and someday I hope to revise it as a poem for public consumption. It would be like a PSA for California drivers about how to use the right and left lanes on a two-lane highway. Maybe it's a utopian poem, a bit unrealistic, but if everyone just did what they were supposed to, if everyone had the same amount of self-awareness and ability to read the cars around them, if everyone drove *exactly just like me*, then this utopia could be possible and we'd all be happy driving on the I-5.

Licht was composed over twenty-six years. It uses electronic and acoustic music, noise, and vocal operatics to tell a loose story involving three characters—Eve, Michael, and Lucifer—gesturing toward mythology, the Bible, The Urantia Book, metaphysical and scientific phenomena, and the cosmos. It is highly mathematical and obsessively structured. Stockhausen goes out of his way to make sure everyone knows he is the genius. He controls everything about *Licht* (and his many other works) and even grooms a few of his children to follow in his footsteps to be sure that, even in death, he can through his offspring maintain some semblance of control.

The piece of writing that begins above, as a previous version of this one, contains many of the same elements. Hue, Venn, Seldom, the whole crew is there, gathering on the ridge above the ocean. I am in the desert. There is no Evan or gay bar; instead, there is Stockhausen and *Licht*.

On the drive to the desert, as I have already said, I listen to *Samstag aus Licht* and overall I dislike it, though I listen to its entirety while driving on the frustrating stretch of the 5 because I remain intrigued. On the same drive I also listen to Earl Sweatshirt's *Some Rap Songs*, which runs for twenty-four minutes in total. I listen to *Some Rap Songs* over and over because it's so pleasurable and short. Thirteen of the fifteen tracks are less than two minutes each. It's so rich you only need a taste to find everything. He says in a Pitchfork interview, "I don't want to waste people's time...I'm trying to say a lot of shit...It can be overwhelming and have an air of exclusivity to it, a pompousness that I feel is only balanced out by me being like, *I know what I'm doing to you.* So I'ma sprint for you. I'ma act like your time is valuable." After *Some Rap Songs* he puts out FEET OF CLAY, just fifteen minutes in total, and I'm struck all over again. I want to be more like Sweatshirt. I fear I am too much like Stockhausen.

Evan's jawline cascades past the pasture and slopes down into the valley. Chase stands at the ridge—the edge of an ear. Tall trees line the crest in the distance. He can't see beyond the boundary of the trees but he knows he will have to get past them. Chase is a spot in the expanse, an ant. He holds a walking stick as he continues the hike. He can see a clearing beyond, where a large lake sits in the valley.

Hue takes cautious steps along the path on Evan's cheek, brushing through the weeds and reaching an overlook where they can see how much further there is to go. Chase is walking behind Hue on the trail, raises his eyes past the back of their head to scan the trees atop the ridge in the distance, looking for the rest of the group that is gathered waiting for their arrival, again, at the mouth of the cave.

This is what happens when you leave the heart of your writing in the desert. Venn pulls the glasses off her face and lays them on the table as she utters the words directly at Seldom, locking with his eyes.

I remove the Karlheinz Stockhausen and add an Evan Kennedy, Seldom says. Then I bring Stockhausen back in as a secondary layer to point to where it came from, I add. Hue yells from the other room: I replace *Licht* with a gay bar and bring in a touch of Earl. Evan gulps his beer.

Suddenly the scaffolding holds. The frame needs feeling. When I add Evan, it becomes a story about composition and friendship.

The desert rejects most things, but when it accepts you, there is your heart lying in the valley, there are your bones holding the scene intact.

I place my hands on either side of Evan's head and the top of his skull opens. I drop the people inside. Little poets for Evan. When he raises the glass of beer to his mouth, the cave howls. Samuel flicks his lighter as a warning that the detonation equipment is ready. I nod. Evan's pupils flare bright red and come back to rest their gaze on the bar. The wind flutters his eyelashes as he says to me: *You are one of the tardy ones.* I smile at my friend.

Hue sighs and signals it's time to leave. Seldom grabs his hat from the stool and sets it lightly on his head. Venn slurps with a straw what's left of her cocktail. Evan hops up and reaches for his backpack as I grab my jacket and push my arms through the sleeves. We walk outside and hug each other goodbye. "It was really good to see you." Then I walk to my train and Evan walks to his.

The ridge above the ocean is motionless for now. Tomorrow I may rip the figures away from Evan, as I tore them from Stockhausen two weeks ago. But alas, perhaps we will settle here a while, at the opening of the cave where our friends await us eagerly to offer something new. A reading one may deliver into a microphone where Evan's tip toes might sing through the voice that I garble. A story there.

I wake early and open the trailer door to a view of the sunrise. I step outside to greet the land. The silence of the desert turns me inward.

A short distance away, behind metal pipes, a bloody organ throbs against the pale light. I hear the crushing of hard dirt under my boots as I walk toward it. I crouch down to poke it with a stick. I lift it with my hand, up to the mouth, rest the tip of my tongue against the pulsing clump, soft and sweet. It slides along my tongue and down, gulped into the belly, a desert song.

The Note

As I walk home from work, my head hangs, my shoulders slump.
It is 2006 in Oakland, California, and I always walk like I'm rushed
to get to where I'm going
hunched and looking down at the ground
I see a note on the sidewalk
It reminds me of a note someone once wrote to me

There's a knock at the door. It's my neighbors who I've never
spoken to. I am in Portland, Oregon in 2001. A note hangs from
their hand. Is this yours? I take it and say thanks. The neighbors
ask if I'm okay. I say I'm fine—it was just a joke. They seem
genuinely concerned for my wellbeing.

Seldom looks up from beneath a layer of sludge
I look down and try to catch his eye, but what can we say to each
other, a double vision intercepted by ripples on the surface of a
pond—?

I look down at the note in my hand. At the time, my girlfriend had
not yet punched me in the head, strangled me, or kicked me while
I was on the ground. She hadn't yet taken the alarm clock cord
and wound it around my neck, pulling the wire tight. I hadn't yet
called the cops because I thought she was going to kill me and had
no other way out.

Something in the neighbors' face warned me about something in the note. Something I didn't see in the note but saw in their face, and then promptly forgot upon closing the door.

It's filthy, Seldom, Venn says. But they want the filth and animals too. Make it funny, a little pathetic, so they chuckle through the filter of your self-narration. Is it 2018? They need to know your politics are in the right place. And that you suffer in all the right ways. Otherwise you can't be the star in your own mirror.

Don't you wish you were born in a different era, among mounting beasts, cavalry raising dirt under their hoofs, beside the trenches where you lay? Venn asks, a smirk in her lips as she peers over her glasses. Seldom shakes his head.

Did I say that? Did I ask how the text is like a slaughtered animal?

I wrote a book that contained an "I" character that was never stable—sometimes a woman, sometimes a man, sometimes an ungendered person or person with an unmarked gender, sometimes a person who was a gender other than what was perceived. The character finds themself in a variety of environments, carrying out experiments. The book felt cogent to me at the time, but I can see now how it starts and stops. The central character is fairly inaccessible, and the changing landscape never seems to settle. It doesn't quite carry you through.

When I get home from work at the coffee shop, I say hi to my cat and quickly make some food to eat. Then I walk to the bar and start drinking.

The bar I refer to is the White Horse Inn, the oldest continually running gay bar in the country, the bar where Jack Spicer used to drink. I go there almost every night and drink too much. It is 2008, and I'm writing a piece called "The line curves where you live" about living on the border of Oakland and Berkeley. It's also about my exploits as a person who drinks too much and sleeps with a lot of people, about the disintegration of a relationship and the desperation I felt and all the sleeping around, the drinking and drugs, the woman twelve years older than me who I was obsessed with for many years and who I started dating in Portland in 2005, just before moving to Oakland, and how things quickly ended after I moved. I wrote about all that too.

I couldn't stand the piece. It was so direct, too vulnerable. I wasn't ready for sentences.

So I decided to chop it up. For every three words, I removed one word. I had no idea how the piece would turn out, but the practice was cathartic. I felt a thrilling rush as I read the piece for the first time all the way through.

Janice left in 2002 after nine months of dating me, eight of them abusive. I spent a lot of time at the E-Room (The Egyptian Club, the now-gone lesbian bar in Portland), which you could say was the precursor to my White Horse days. Dark gay bar with outdated décor, pool tables, karaoke nights, and a dance room. I would drink Jameson on the rocks and smoke Camel lights and wear a leather jacket and shoot pool. There was something very deep inside me that felt satisfied by this as a way of life. It felt destructive, but real, like I was accessing a secret, like desire. I chopped off my hair for the second time. I read *Stone Butch Blues* for the first time. I tried using a packer, it didn't feel right. I flinched when my new girlfriend would make a sudden motion. I smoked inside the bar. I kept my eyes on everyone.

Was it a book of prose that should have been verse? Or vice versa?

It was not an easy decision for me to start taking hormones or get top surgery. Certainly not as easy as removing one word for every three, bringing the form and content together in a way that worked.

Seldom walks beside Hue. His hands are in his pockets. Hue drops back and kicks Seldom's ankle to the side as he takes a step. He stumbles and jerks up. They laugh. Seldom is surprised to see Hue in this way, jovial and light-footed. They have a boyish look, pretty, with something heavy and dark in there. He feels bashful around them. They walk with their hands in their pockets, talking about a book they're reading, already on to the next subject but he's still somewhere before, not thinking, just an ambient sort of processing in the back of his mind that keeps him distracted from being present.

It wasn't the village they strolled through
On a path that led them back here once again
The story for someone to see—written once from above, then beside
From beneath the sludge he looks up, then back down to the page
Which verses are the ones that caught you looking?
Seldom signs his name at the bottom of the page.

Every five or ten years, I find myself thumbing through old journals. Usually it's when I'm moving. And this is the day in my packing where I don't do any. Instead, I read through the old journals and notebooks, the old folders stuffed with writing from my younger years. Sometimes I skip over the two journals that cover the nine months when I dated Janice. In these pages things go dark. The appearance of my writing changes, letters look sharper, more angular, written with a depressed and frantic energy, the pen impressions are deeper in the page. I flip forward and see the pages where we scribble words and drawings together about her abusive behavior—our way of talking about it. I can see myself sitting next to Janice in the Red & Black Café on Division Street in Portland, drawing an image of myself with welts all over my head as she adds captions that explain why I deserve them.

The Red & Black was an anarchist collective coffee shop and gathering space a few blocks from where I lived in Southeast Portland. It was 2001. I just moved to town. Morgan gave me free bowls of chili when I was broke. I used their computers to check my Hotmail account. The Red & Black hosts open mic poetry nights. It's one of the first places I read my work aloud. One night before a reading, I'm sitting on the ground outside in a hoodie smoking a cigarette. Walt Curtis stops in front of me and asks if I'm a homeless boy. I say no. He turns and walks inside.

I move back to the neighborhood on the border of Oakland and Berkeley, into a blue house with my partner, at the end of 2017. I walk to the Nomad coffee shop, where I would go almost every day when I first arrive in this neighborhood from 2005 to 2010 just over there, in the studio apartment on Telegraph and

Alcatraz. Nomad is the coffee shop where I write "the line curves where you live." Now, I write here in the same coffee shop about that piece, how I cut one word for every three words and made it better. I walk on the same streets but my head no longer hangs, my shoulders are less slumped. I walk a little less rushed. I'm still the same person, same anxieties and fears, same delusions, but I have more presence and intention, more inner stillness. This is partly because I transitioned, but it's also because I grew up. I did the work. When I am pushed on a stretcher into an operating room or begin to insert a needle into my body once a week, I receive many congratulations. I want to say: if you could see what it took me to get there. But that story is mine.

My first book was an accurate representation of where I was at the time of writing it. Now I long to tell another story—one that may jump around in time and contradict, that may draw from real and imaginary landscapes of people and environments, that has unstable subjects and speakers—where everyone in the home is stranded and together—a reflection of my embodied state today.

Chase pokes out from a huge pile of leaves. Hue looks at him through the window as they wipe their hands on a towel. Venn comes up the stairs from the basement and stands in the doorway, tapping her foot. She's giving Samuel a call but he doesn't answer. Samuel is wading in the swamp, moving his arms around to catch the composition. When he brings pieces back in a bucket, Seldom will wash them off. I place them in my mouth one by one to feel out their potential and decide what goes in and what stays out. Chase rakes the leaves into a pile so he can jump into them again. Venn goes back downstairs.

To release the self from words
—words, a mere representation—
to walk the life that is yours
with the breath that is yours

I remember being pleased to be mistaken for a boy. Not only by
Walt Curtis, but any time it happened. I was just beginning to be a
lesbian, a dyke, in those early Portland years. I felt a kind of pride
to be seen as male—a marker of my dykedom. I still feel like a ten-
der-hard butch sometimes. Sometimes I feel soft, like a young girl
or boy. Sometimes I feel scruffy and toned, like a man. The iden-
tifying words hold something, but they mean nothing without the
lives that fill them. I use new words, have a new form, but I don't
renounce the previous iterations of myself, even those no longer
visible. Every version of this book lives inside it. The "I" is a coag-
ulation of timestamps resisting a wholly integrated present. The
present is always complete in its shattered aspect.

When Janice brings me to the emergency room, a nurse asks
her to leave for a moment and hands me some pamphlets about
domestic violence. Then she sends me home with Janice. After
another sleepless night of punching and strangling and raping, I
go to work at the natural food store—originally a local shop called
Natures, which gets bought out by Wild Oats, which gets bought
out by Whole Foods, which gets bought out by Amazon. But here,
I am working at the deli counter of Wild Oats, early one morning
in 2002, when Janice walks in. She says to me over the counter
that her car is packed and she's driving to Los Angeles for good. I
stand there, stunned, in my little white cap and apron as she turns
and walks away.

I am free from her in that moment. But not of my own doing. This is two weeks before we're supposed to move in together. If she had not left me when she did—

The building is starting to disintegrate. We are going to let it be so

Coasting through the streets of the village, after writing something that wanted to show up in a certain way, but didn't. After I sat myself down on the curb and wondered. How would I ever come to write about myself in this way—?

And Seldom says,

how the building comes to be the story / we tell through your window

He had forgotten about the piece he was trying to write a few years ago, in which the text was a dead body, a slaughtered animal.

A book to be prose. Or could it be verse?

The body / of work
holds its previous versions inside
—invisible and present—
building its aura out of them

I reach my hand into the swamp and pluck Seldom out, my arm dripping with mud and saliva, blood and gunk. The stuff of old writing, old bodies, old selves and thoughts, desires and trauma, the old versions of us—

every body's got them

A note lying on the sidewalk

I'm in Forestville, working on the book. When I arrive I pull out
a container of disinfectant wipes and scrub all surfaces thor-
oughly—the doorknobs, the light switches, everything. It's risky to
travel in the first place. Everything is shut down from the global
pandemic. COVID-19 has torn through the social fabric of our
lives. We've been in quarantine for months, four hundred million
jobless, death everywhere.

George Floyd was killed by police. It is Juneteenth and people
are at a port shutdown in Oakland. Rage and togetherness swirl
through streets across the country, on the internet, through our
minds as we imagine a different world. Angela Davis and Ruth
Wilson Gilmore are widely quoted on the internet and invited
to give talks as Black youth lead marches, topple statues, call for
prison abolition and defunding the police.

I talk with Charity on the phone because it's her birthday. She's
amped up from being out there. She says these kids don't need to
spend years reading political theory and sitting in endless meetings. They're fired up. Born ready. It's time.

Something keeps getting in the way of the book. I'm taking stock
of the year, of the years. It seems we're in another long transition, lasting for decades, centuries, millennia, time on any scale, it
doesn't matter. We're smack in the middle of something. It's hard
to see what it is. Today is Friday.

Trisha is nine years younger than me. She opens me up to things I was closed to, like pop culture, bad television, and Twitter. These things I considered superficial "trash" for years—products that masses tumble into addictively, that strengthen capitalism's mental hold. I resisted, choosing instead to immerse myself in art made in the dark cultural crevices. Now, I learn how to learn through mass-consumed stuff too. I don't feel threatened by it. I can enjoy it and maintain my connection to the underworld. I can poke my head up and look around, take it in, learn from what's happening out there. I've learned something about the value of pleasure. I've learned many other things from Trisha, too. And she from me, I can tell.

I've been so humbled by my mental breakdown that all I can do is stay open to learning and let myself be. I continue to struggle with feeling unseen—just like everyone, I suppose. I spend a lot of time questioning my values against the values of others, just like everyone. I need external validation, just like everyone. I try not use the internet as validation since the effects are, at best short-lived, and at worst the opposite of what I seek. It's lonely either way.

This time last year, I'm just getting out of the hospital. I do an intensive outpatient program at Kaiser. I return to therapy. I get on meds. I return to my qigong practice. I try things out. Take a landscape horticulture class at Merritt College and tend to the garden. Take a certification class in mediation and conflict resolution at SEEDS. Start working at Small Press Traffic. I go to the East Bay Meditation Center and sit for two twenty-minute sits, separated by two strikes of a bell. At the beginning of the practice, the rotating leader of this peer-led group quotes Mushim: "Our hearts are broken, our community is whole." Trisha and I work on repairing our relationship. It takes a year, but we return to a place of closeness and trust, stronger than before. I write a lot, but it's all process writing. Working on the book feels impossible. I am too tender for words. I am broken, but whole.

I look at the notebook that I took outside with me after downing the bottle of pills. It's a letter to Trisha. It says there are women approaching me. They gather around slowly—not rushing in. They feel warm. They look calm. I tell her not to worry, I will be okay. My handwriting trails off into unreadable scribbles.

In 2020, my cat Sisa, who lived with me for seventeen years, dies in April. I spend a week with my grandmother Ruth after my grandfather Norman dies in July at the age of ninety-two. Later in the year, fires will break out again in California. For two weeks, the sky will be covered in smoke, a haze of white and gray. Ash plumes swirl into the car when the door opens. It is eerily silent—as in, the birds are silent. I check the fire map on my phone and flame icons sweep across the state, up into Oregon. There's a heat wave but we can't open windows because the air quality is too poor. Like almost everyone else, we don't have air conditioning, so we swelter in our closed-up homes, amidst the pandemic. I think about the tens of thousands of houseless people throughout the state of California who are breathing this air without protection. I check the AQI monitor on my phone daily. It hovers in red and purple, pushes up into deep purple and slides back down to red—"very unhealthy air" it says—then, eventually, down to orange and yellow. Soon it will be back in the green, won't it?

Then one day, the sky is completely obscured by smoke in a way that causes the light to glow orange—the strangest thing I've ever seen. Instagram fills with images of real-life sci-fi apocalyptic movie stills. It's right outside.

Then my friend Cassie dies in October, a few days before her fortieth birthday. Cassie. I put my hand to my heart.

Then Trump contests the election. Twitter is a nightmarish hellhole that no one can look away from.

It is a year later, again, since then. Thursday, June 16, 2021. I'm staying in a little cabin in the woods of Point Arena. It has been two years since my manic episode, at the retreat house just five miles from here. I've been writing every day since I arrived. I'm reading books and watching films. I'm shooting video. I paint on postcard-sized paper with my new watercolor set. I walk seven miles at the Stornetta Public Lands. I drive up Highway 1, turn outside Elk on County Road 132, slither over to Philo and hike six miles through Hendy Woods State Park. I go back through old versions of the book. I discover in an old file that Seldom's name, in his first appearance in a poem, was Sed. Sed means "thirst."

I'm trying to finish the book. It'll never be what it wanted to be. The stuff of life got in the way. But books never end up exactly as they are dreamed. Neither do our selves. Neither do our struggles. But we write them, we make them, we do them. We do our best.

Today was the day

we were going to make it

all the way over to there

before we knew it—

"They should've done it differently"

"It was never there in the first place"

The ground drops out
shaky ground

Nothing ever waits for you to take it

sometimes vampires lurk in the dark waiting for your thickest
vein

and you *would have done it differently*

Still can, someone says, but you hadn't heard them say it

didn't get the memo

things being what they are

in algorithms and scenes

it's not so easy to—

listen

A sun rises and sets   every seventeen seconds

—in your hand

In the dark

someone waits for a vein to suck

another licks what spills out on its own

someone else is tending to their wounds

When I no longer remember the situation that I describe

but keep describing it anyway

letting some other thing come in to inform, take over

—the narrative

of the first that had gotten lost because I stopped

writing for a few months between the first version and the second

the missing part, this absence, getting filled and maybe for the better

defying coherence within the frame

As I want to tell you a story of a world

imagined, as the real thing, you could get it

being in that closed system yourself

But also to tell a story of this world

to those in the beyond

as time stretches lengthwise

covering experience

Everything has already been done, they say

for instance, when I got here, I told myself something would happen

then something else happened

I didn't let go of the first thought, I held onto it

And later I looped back to let it happen, then I wrote about it

so as not to forget the occurrences

If I look at the networks for too long

tossed this way and that—

things can always be differently arranged, is that something they say?

So you consider becoming an arranger

leaving space for whoever has quickness

of mind and fingers, time and investments,

an ability to generate the right kind of thing

when writing is not coming easy

to take time, and focus, a patience that's hard to hold

I think about giving it up, spend time with plants instead

or do something more useful, like help people that are suffering in
the city where I live

But the drive is still there

still I need to get it down

it is a commitment made long ago

to the histories of absence

that stretch across time in all directions

the burden of every passing year

with the world being what it is

more so they say these days

I'm not so sure

I talk with one friend and another

about writing and living as a writer

I say something about directing intentionality

if that is what you want

whether or not the writing happens

how in my case it is not, or how slowly it goes—

and being reminded that I once said

reading and thinking are part of the process of writing,

a way of living, a way of being

Part of the history of absence—

the mystery swirling beneath the story of progress

a romantic notion, I wonder

As I continue to work on this book

and complain to everyone about how long it takes me

I remind myself that there is all the time in the world

however long it takes

and also that I need to step on the gas

if I want to get all the books out of me

that I know are there (at least three)

The narration is to bounce around

as context tightens around your thought

which is the zone of the terrible world, again?

And why would anyone want to be there

when there are all these other places you could go

I had a way of talking and it ended

the way of talking was to keep the message buried underneath

but where are the diggers—

hidden, everywhere

when I return to the subject behind the poem

how we were attempting to get somewhere

—never getting close

whether the ground was there or not

shaky or firm

or whoever else was there or not

and for whatever reasons

To find myself spun around

the interior of the poem

which is the interior of myself

in a vortex of the world spinning

and feel the genome tighten

a history of such things

the ways of us

Histories absent, the history of absence

poets know this—

time is longer than all of your words

Sometimes I get so resentful

with the ones I love most

wanting to fight

so I can know my own boundaries

never so clear for me

and remembering that everyone else is doing the same

circles upon circles

a rings-of-hell existence

in friendship and love—with fury hope sadness longing

a desire to destroy what holds us back

from being, and from being together

in the meantime—

We bleed all the time

some slurp up the drops on the surface

others pretend they don't notice

what's seeping onto the pavement

from their own gashes and wounds

—you always point to something else, it's never you—

they pretend not to notice

that we are the ones who are hungry

Most of the time

I am

Acknowledgments

Parts of this book have been previously published by *A Perfect Vacuum*, *Amerarcana: A Bird & Beckett Review* #6 and #8, *Necessary Failures*, *The Believer*, *The Elephants*, *Social Text*, and *Tripwire*. Thank you to the editors.

Deep appreciation to friends who gave valuable feedback: Maxe Crandall, Evan Kennedy, Trisha Low, Pamela Lu, Juliana Spahr, Violet Spurlock, Stephanie Young. To Jocelyn Saidenberg for believing in this work. To all my friends for your love and support.

To the members of my two writing groups, so grateful for your thoughts and feedback on this writing and more, and for sharing your work with me.

This book was carefully edited by the incisive Broc Rossell. Thank you.

Always to my sister, Alana Staiti

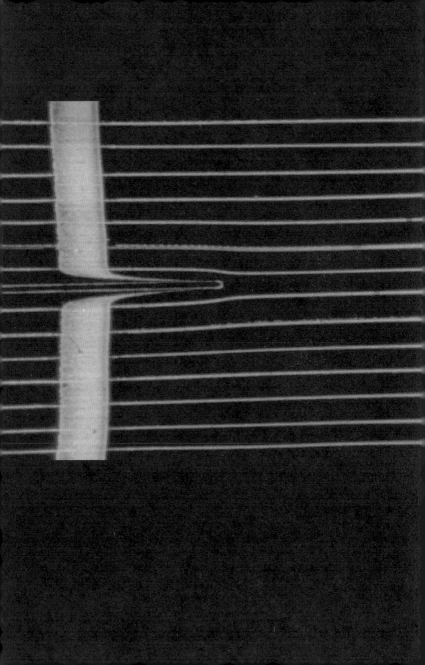